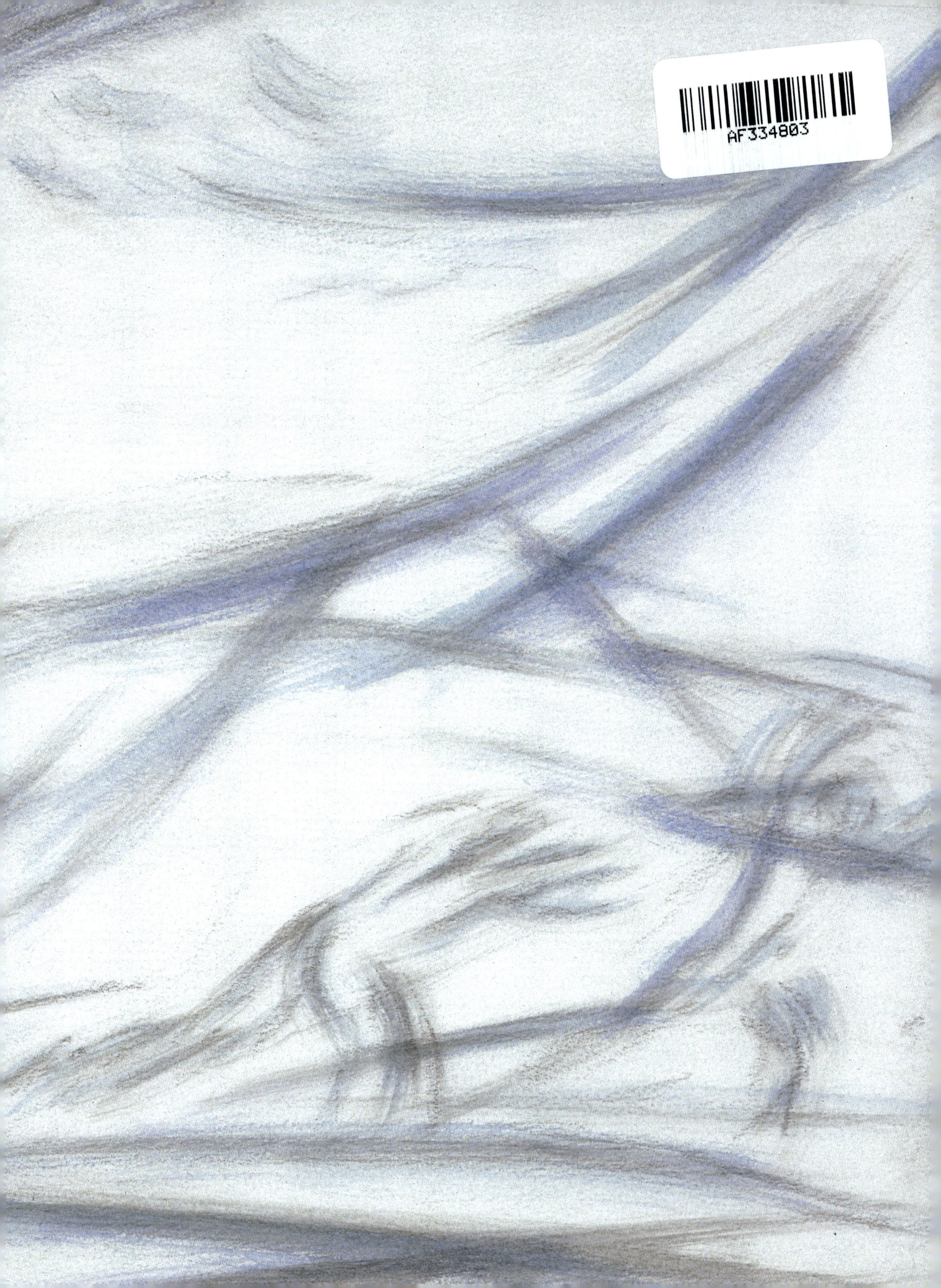

LORSER FEITELSON

THE KINETIC SERIES - WORKS FROM 1916 - 1923

LORSER FEITELSON

THE KINETIC SERIES - WORKS FROM 1916 - 1923

SEPTEMBER 10 - DECEMBER 23 2005

Louis Stern Fine Arts

9002 Melrose Avenue
West Hollywood, CA 90069
T 310-276-0147 F 310-276-7740
gallery@louisstern.com
www.louissternfinearts.com

CONTENT

ACKNOWLEDGMENT

It is most fitting that this, our second in a series of exhibitions chronicling the life and work of Lorser Feitelson, should be a radical departure from the first. In retrospect, focusing on Feitelson's initial experiments with form, composition and motion, I find myself all the more dazzled by his work's nervy evolution from representational to surrealist to hard edge.

Feitelson's introduction, courtesy of the Armory show of 1913, to the extraordinary visual revolution generated by European modernists, greatly influenced him as well as many of his American contemporaries. His ability to absorb and reinterpret these new ideas in his work attests not only to his talent for artistic re-invention but also to his enduring openness to fresh inquiries into the nature of art itself. In many ways, Feitelson's passion for this "new" art from Europe, while aligning himself to these European visionaries, also put him and his contemporaries at the forefront of the development of American painting in the twentieth century.

Again, as with the previous exhibition, in sifting through his volume of sketches, drawings and studies, I am greatly impressed by the audacity and range of his work. While his contributions as a scholar, teacher, lecturer and collector are acknowledged, it is a great privilege to be a part of the re-discovery of Feitelson as an early innovator.

I would like to thank Wendy Van Haerlem and the Feitelson Arts Foundation for their support and assistance in this exhibition. Their continued commitment and generosity simply make everything easier. For this I am deeply grateful.

Tamara Devrient has served as our liaison with the Feitelson Arts Foundation and has co-coordinated all the various aspects of this publication. Her passion and dedication to the project has been of invaluable assistance to me and my staff.

I would also like to express my appreciation to Peter Selz for his thought-provoking and insightful essay. Finally, I would like to thank my staff: Marie Chambers, Deborah Stern and Jennifer Ward. I could not do it without them, and for their involvement I am sincerely grateful.

Louis Stern

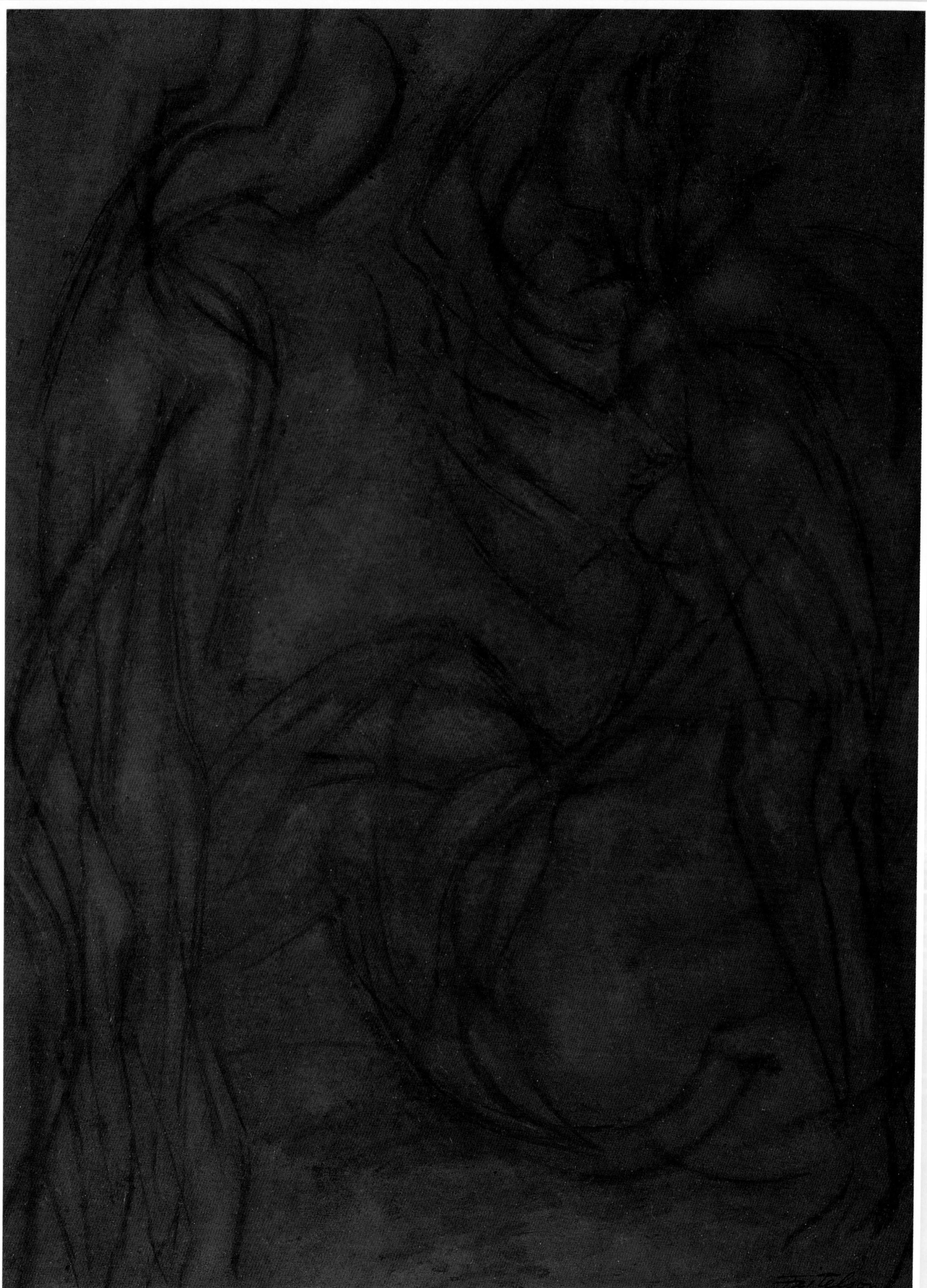

In 1913 the fifteen-year-old Lorser Feitelson was inspired by the Armory Show in New York to become a painter. He was not totally unprepared for this experience. Born in Savannah, Georgia in 1898 and brought up in New York, he had drawing lessons from his father, saw reproductions of paintings by the masters--Michelangelo, Titian, Tintoretto--and was taken to the Metropolitan Museum to see the real thing. At the age of twelve he began to paint in oils. But seeing the International Exhibition of Modern Art at the Armory, located at Lexington and 25th Street, was a revelation. The show displayed the new art from Europe, which astonished the public and many of the more traditional American artists. Although Alfred Stieglitz had been exhibiting avant-garde European art as well as American pioneers at 291 Fifth Avénue, his Photo-Secession Gallery was an intimate place only for the select few. At the Armory, a vast display of "Modern Art" from Goya and Ingres to Brancusi and Duchamp astounded the visitors. Based on the 1912 Sonderbund Exhibition in Cologne, it was a massive enterprise.

PETER SELZ THE KINETIC WORKS BY LORSER FEITELSON

At the Armory Show, the American public was introduced to a presentation of Post-Impressionists with 17 works by Van Gogh, 14 by Cézanne, 13 by Gauguin, and 5 by Toulouse-Lautrec. There were no works by Seurat, but 3 by Signac were exhibited. Odilon Redon was featured with 30 works and Matisse with 17. Unlike the Sonderbund Exhibition, the Armory show lacked works by the Russian avant-garde. There were very few German Expressionists, but Kandinsky's *Improvisation No. 27* was there. It was displayed in a dark spot, so that the critics paid little attention to the most abstract painting in the exhibition, but it was purchased by Stieglitz and thus available for viewing by young American artists. The Cubists were represented with 8 works by Picasso, one by Braque, and the artists of the Section d'Or, including the Duchamp brothers.

The show was highly controversial, if not disconcerting. Most of the press took umbrage at the Europeans at the Armory. The Cubists, according to one established critic, were "either a clever hoax or negligible pedantry." But most of the anger was directed at Matisse and at Marcel Duchamp for their willful distortions of the human form. Harriet Monroe, the poet and celebrated editor of *Poetry* magazine, described Matisse's paintings as "the most hideous monstrosity ever perpetrated in the name of long suffering art." To be sure, Monroe became a bit more tolerant after several viewings when the show was in Chicago. Duchamp's *Nude Descending a Staircase (1912)* was the focal point of the attack. It was called "The Rude Descending a Staircase (Rush Hours at the Subway)" and "Explosion in a Shingle Factory" and much else. But it was undoubtedly the paintings by Matisse and Duchamp as well as Picabia's dynamic *Dances at the Spring* that exerted the greatest impression on the young Lorser Feitelson.

The Italian Futurists were absent from the Armory, presumably because they wanted to exhibit only as a group. But viewers and critics of the exhibition, uncertain about art-historical definitions, thought of Duchamp and Picabia as Futurists. And with Marinetti's genius for publicity, work by the Futurists was no means unknown in America, even prior to their notable presence at the Panama-Pacific Exposition, the San Francisco World's Fair of 1915. Several New York artists had established contact with the vanguard European artists. John Marin, who was in Europe from 1905 to 1910, was probably the first American painter to incorporate dynamic principles in his paintings. When he returned to New York, he produced paintings of the Woolworth Building and the Brooklyn Bridge with, what he called, their "warring, pushing, pulling forces." Marin was represented with ten of these dynamic paintings in the Armory Show.

Max Weber's canvases such as *Rush Hour (1915)* and *Chinese Restaurant (1915)* are paintings that reveal his personal friendship with the avant-garde artists of Paris, where he worked from 1905 to 1909. While Joseph Stella was in Paris in 1912, he saw the Futurist show at Bernheim-Jeune. He was familiar with the 1909 and 1910 Futurist manifestos and was personally acquainted with Carlo Carrà and probably also with Umberto Boccioni and Gino Severini.

Stella's two still lifes that were hung in the Armory were still quite traditional, but his work after the show such as *Battle of Lights, Coney Island (1913)* with its faceted sweeping form and its kaleidoscopic sifting of color and its dazzling energy is a painting that manifests the presence of Futurism in America. Its impact is also apparent in the diagonal rays of light and simultaneous viewpoints in the watercolors and canvases by Charles Demuth; similar shafts of light appear in the stunning landscapes and cityscapes by the American expatriate Lyonel Feininger who saw Futurist paintings at the Sturm Gallery in Berlin in 1912 and produced his prismatic paintings such as *Bicycle Racer (1912)* and *Sidewheeler (1913)* under the impact of Futurism. Lorser Feitelson's Futurist paintings, which he named "Kinetic Studies," must be seen in this context.

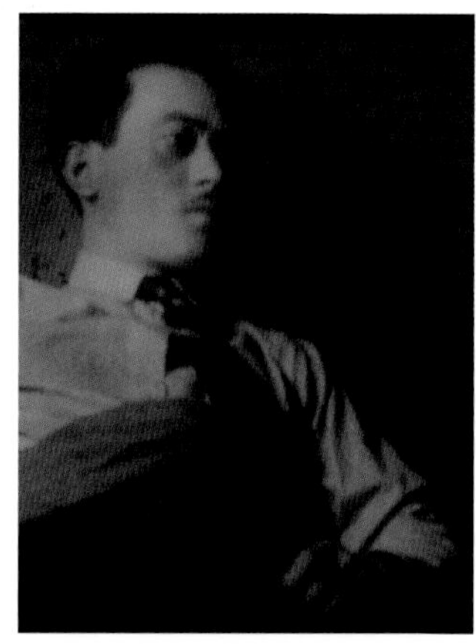

Lorser Feitelson, circa 1925

Prior to his precocious paintings, which can now be seen as belonging to the American avant-garde, he was immersed in the New York art world of the time. In 1916 he moved into a studio in Greenwich Village and a year later relocated to a studio above the bohemian Penguin Club and also became a member of the Whitney Club on Eighth Street. He met Charles Demuth, Andrew Dasburg, and Charles Sheeler as well as the organizers of the Armory Show, Arthur B. Davies and Walter Pach and the American realists Robert Henri and John Sloan. The English Vorticist Wyndam Lewis, working in a dynamic Futurist mode, was an acquaintance, and he befriended Jules Pascin, who had been represented with twelve works on paper at the Armory and was best known for his erotic drawings, done with a spontaneous elegant line. Pascin was born in Bulgaria, went to Germany and lived in Paris for many years. He knew all the artists there and was helpful to Feitelson, when the young American artist decided to go to Paris to study drawing at the Académie Colarossi, where he was an independent student for a year, returning to New York in 1920. This was his only formal training in art. Some of the "Kinetic Studies" appear to have been made during that year in Paris.

During that time Feitelson also became cognizant of the new literature on avant-garde art. He had Arthur Jerome Eddy's *Cubists and Post-Impressionists* in his library. Published in 1914, it was the first book in English on the new art with chapters on "Les Fauves", Cubism, "The New Art in Munich," "Color Music," and Futurism. In this book Eddy printed translations of excerpts of the Futurist manifestos as well as reproductions of paintings by Balla, Boccioni and Severini.

When Lorser Feitelson made his "Kinetic Studies," he was in command of an active visual archive and of many aspects of the theories of modernist art. A painting such as *Figure, 1918-20 (Plate 10)* is a composition closely related to the analytical Cubism of Braque and Picasso, who dissected and depersonalized their figures for the sake of new formal construction, while still providing clues to the actual model. Feitelson here also adopted the muted monochromes, the brownish-gray tones of the Cubists, but added dippled textures to achieve an animated surface.

The *Kinetic Figures* of *1919-20 (Plates 23 and 24)* are solidly constructed paintings. The bodies in both panels are faceted and simplified. Painted in orange and black respectively, they are boldly defined and bound in black contour lines. They convey a sense of volume in space reminiscent of Cézanne. Since his Memorial Exhibition at the Salon d'Automne in 1907, the Post-Impressionist master exerted the greatest influence on the painters of the next generation. It was what Arthur Jerome Eddy at the time referred to as "The substance of things painted impressionistically" which absorbed the painters of the early 20th Century. Feitelson's *Bathers #8, 1918-1919 (Plate 8)* is small in dimension but large in scale. Like Cézanne in *The Great Bathers (1906)*, Feitelson fuses the figures with the surrounding landscape. Whereas Cézanne formalized his figures into a domed architectural setting, Feitelson pressed his female bodies into a closer figuration. In addition, his subtle tones of aubergine do not have the combination of sonorous colors in Cézanne's late masterpieces.

A similar integration of bodies--now painted in orange--can be seen in *Figures, 1918-1919 (Plate 7)* or in *Two Bathers (Organized Articulation) (Plate 16)* of the same year, painted in umber tones. In these paintings the artist makes use of the Futurist device of multiple parallel lines to convey sequential movement. The interplay of light and dark in these pivotal works helps create a sense of dynamic activity in the viewer's eye. In the Technical Manifesto of 1910, the Futurists affirmed that "all things move, all things are rapidly changing."[1] Two years later, becoming more specific, they declared that, "what must be rendered is the *dynamic sensation*, that is to say, the particular rhythm of each object, its inclination, its movement, or to put it more exactly, interior force...Every object reveals by its lines how it would resolve itself were it to follow the tendencies of its forces."[2] The awareness that moving objects multiply themselves on the viewer's retina is evident in Balla's well-known *Dynamics of a Dog on a Leash* of 1912 with the skittering legs and feet of both dog and mistress. Feitelson, in his 1919 painting, *Two Nudes and a Cat (Plate 15)* has, as it were, substituted two naked women for the skirt and feet of Balla's lady, and a cat seems to gyrate between the two girls, one of them seated unsteadily in a chair, the other quickly bending toward the twirling cat.

The "Kinetic Paintings" by Feitelson are also related to works by Matisse, such as *Portrait of Mlle. Yvonne Landsberg, 1914* in which striations repeat the curves of the model's shoulders, arms, head, and hips, curved lines which emphasize her body and extend it into space. Artists and intellectuals at the time were engaged in discussions of Henri Bergson's book *Creative Evolution* and its concept of élan vital, which provided a theoretical background for the idea of change and flux that was so essential to the painting of the Cubists, Futurists and also Matisse.

In the same year, Feitelson made a series of panels on the legendary theme of Leda and the Swan. Since the Renaissance, this subject has been the object of paintings of erotic encounter. Zeus, the highest god who could transform himself at will, turned into a swan to make love to the beauteous Leda. This theme provided painters with the opportunity to depict undraped women at play. Leonardo's Leda is lost, but we have a contemporary copy by Cesare de Sesto in which a standing swan is embraced by the nude Leda. Other artists represented Leda in a recumbent position. Highly erotic is Theodore Gericault's *Leda and the Swan*, in which the Romantic painter placed the couple in natural surroundings with Leda leaning against a rock. Her right arm both reaches for and curbs a very large and aggressive swan. A similar encounter appears in Feitelson's *Leda (Study in Kinetics), 1919 (Plate 6)*. In Feitelson's painting, however, Leda has multiple legs, suggesting separate phases of her action simultaneously, while her arm grasps for the expectant swan. In a related work of that year, *Leda, Study in Kinetics (Plate 18)* Leda's arms and torso are further multiplied, and the presence of the swan is only suggested by her extended arm. These panels are painted in tenebristic earth tones with the action occurring in shallow space, bringing the action close to the spectator's eye.

Mother and Child (Bathers, Kinetic Organization), 1919-1920 (Plate 27), painted in the same tones, is a small and eloquent painting of love and trust between mother and child. In the pyramidal composition the young mother, seen in profile, is reaching for her child who is stretching his whole small body toward her. There is a great deal of deep-felt energy expressed in this "kinetic" study in which the Futurist lines of force have become paths of emotion.

During the same period Feitelson also painted a number of still life compositions such as *Pears and Apples (Plate 33)*, which recall still lifes by Cézanne. But in Feitelson's painting, the solid form of the fruit is broken up and finds its place in an ambiguous space in a picture done in bright juicy reds.

Related to the Kinetic Paintings were watercolors and Conte-crayon architectural studies. These works--*New York Buildings, 1919 (Plate 13), Architectural Abstraction-Buildings, 1920 (Plate 29)* and *Interior, 1921 (Plate 34)*--with their angular geometric forms, overlapping planes and their perpendicular and diagonal lines, resemble Lyonel Feininger's early crystalline architectural paintings.

Feitelson's *Two Bathers (Kinetic Study), 1919-20 (Plate 25)* pictures two nudes, painted in orange and bounded by multiple black outlines. Placed in shallow space, the girls are all sharp angles. The picture was probably based on life drawings he did at the Académie Colarossi, but its attenuation of the figures points back to Mannerist painting of the early 16th Century. Mannerism, with its interest in instability and movement, the distortion of the human figure breaking with the perfect proportion of the High Renaissance, the elongated figures crowded

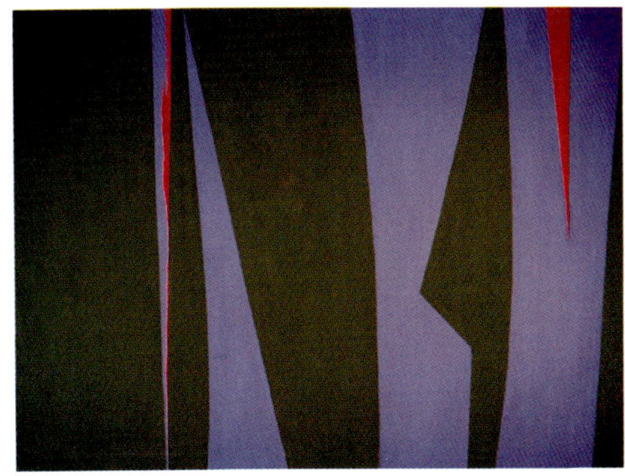

Space Form, 1952

in small spaces, and its subjective expression was of paramount interest to art historians and artists in the early 20th Century, and paintings like Lorser Feitelson's *Two Bathers (Kinetic Study)* clearly indicate a response to the art of painters such as Parmigianino, Rosso Fiorentino or El Greco.

This is a pivotal work also because it points ahead to Feitelson's later work. Following the "Kinetic Studies" and after his move to Los Angeles in 1927, the artist turned to neo-classical figure painting in the 1920s, followed by Post-Surrealism in the '30s, the "Magical Forms" of the 1940s and the "Magical Space Forms" of the 1950s. It was the latter that prompted me in 1957 to organize the exhibition "Abstract Classicism," which included John McLaughlin, Fred Hammersley, and Karl Benjamin together with Feitelson.[3] A work such as *Space Form, 1952*, with its elongated angular shapes, is clearly related to *Two Bathers* of 33 years earlier. Now strong colors-- mostly black and purple--replaced the orange tones of the earlier painting, and the picture space has been flattened further, but the general sensibility is clearly that of the same artist. A "Hard Edge Line Painting" such as *Untitled, 1961*, with its curved dancing lines and rapid movement, carried his work to the next stage. This painting, abstract as it appears, still suggests anatomical--female--references of breasts and buttocks. The human form has become much more distilled, but a painting such as this certainly adhered to the Futurist or kinetic precept that "the gesture...shall simply be dynamic sensation itself."[4]

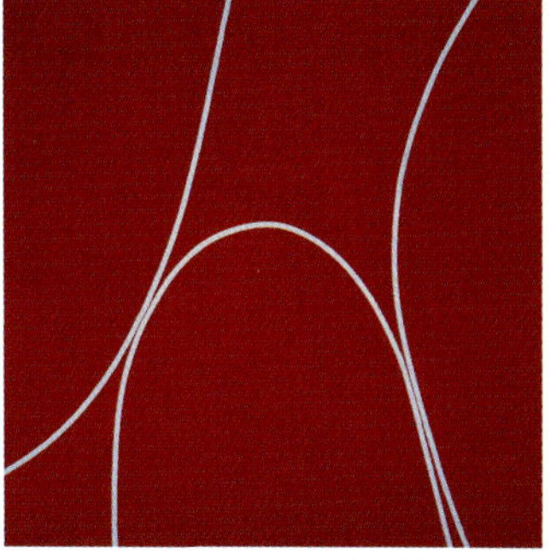

Untitled, 1961

Peter Selz

Peter Selz is professor emeritus of modern art at the University of California, Berkeley, where he was also the founding director of the Berkeley Art Museum. He was previously chief curator of the Department of Painting and Sculpture Exhibitions at New York's Museum of Modern Art. Selz, Corresponding Editor of *Art in America*, is the author of some fifteen books on modern art, the most recent being *The Art of Engagement/Visual Politics in California and Beyond*, to be published by the University of California Press in Fall 2005.

[1] "Futurist Painting: Technical Manifesto" (April 21, 1910) as published in Joshua C. Taylor, *Futurism* (New York, the Museum of Modern Art, 1961), 125.
[2] "The Exhibition and the Public" (February 5, 1912) in Taylor, op.cit. 125.
[3] As I was leaving the Los Angeles area for New York, I asked my friend (and Feitelson's close friend) Jules Langsner to take over. The exhibition, which he called "Four Abstract Classicists," was presented first at the San Francisco Museum of Modern Art and next at the Los Angeles County Museum of Art, as well as in the Institute of Contemporary Art in London and Belfast. In its catalogue Langsner coined the term "Hard Edge."
[4] "Futurist Painting: Technical Manifesto," op.cit. 125.

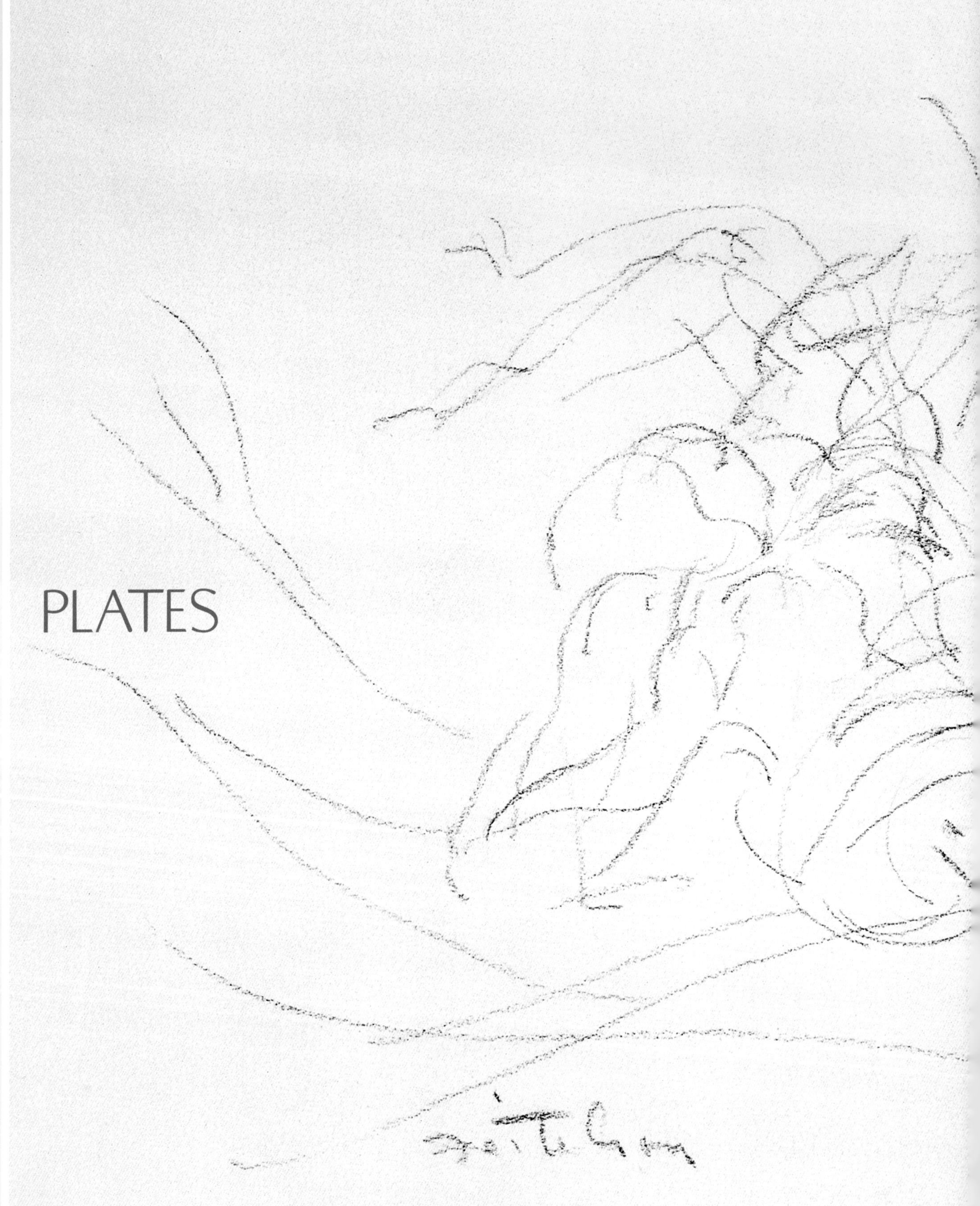

PLATES

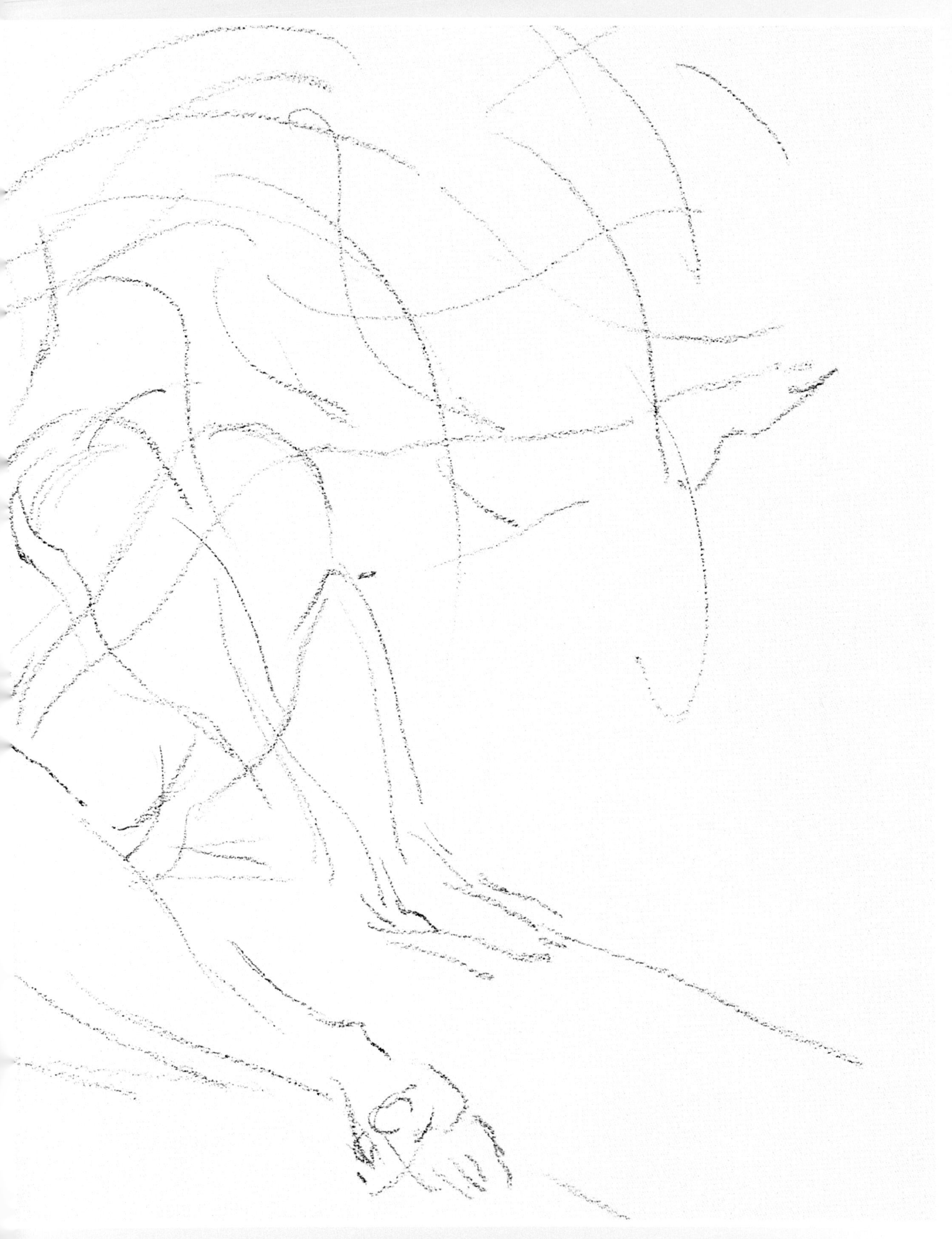

1.

SEATED FIGURE IN ACTION
(KINETIC STUDY)

1917-18
watercolor on carton
10 $^1/_8$ x 13 $^3/_4$ inches
25.7 x 34.9 centimeters

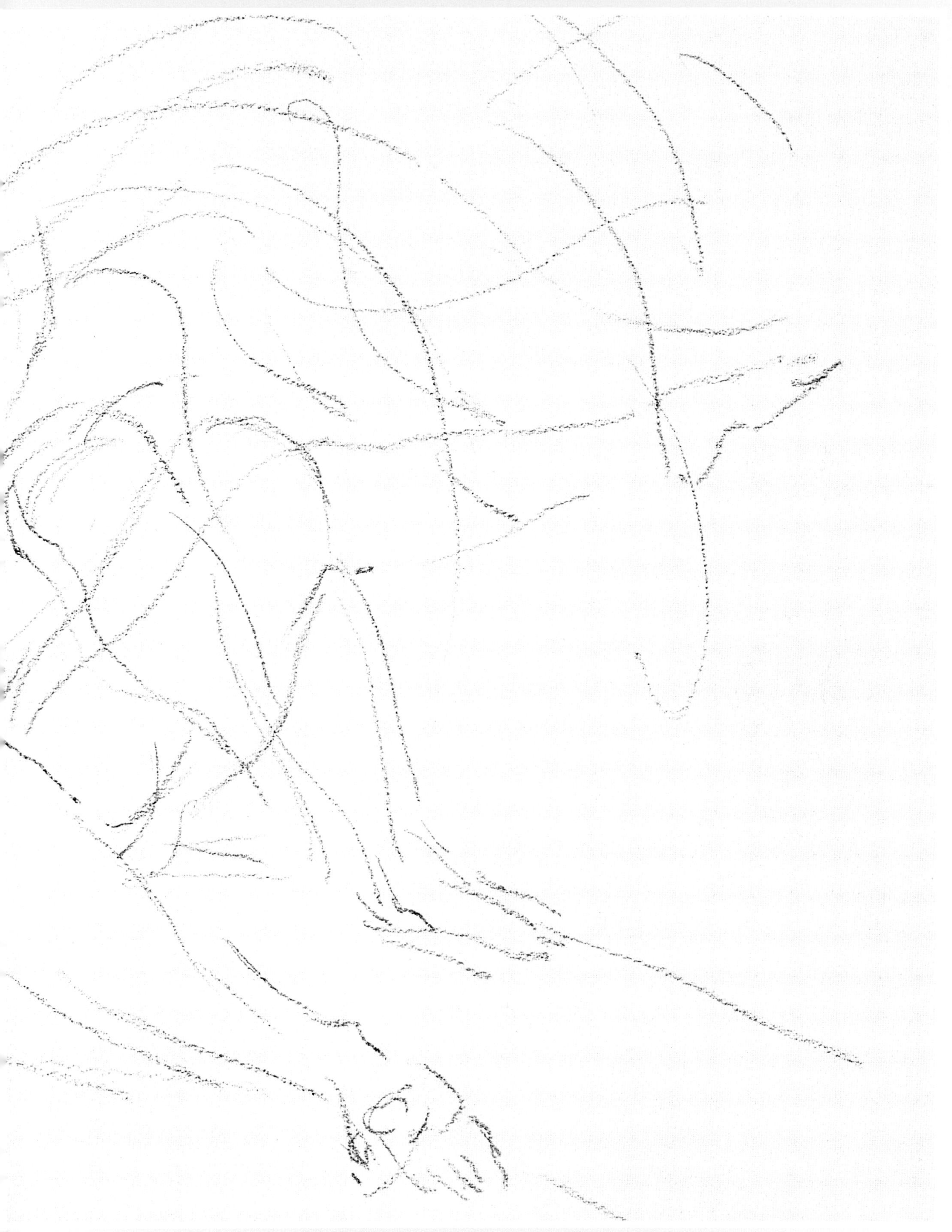

1.

SEATED FIGURE IN ACTION
(KINETIC STUDY)

1917-18
watercolor on carton
10 $^1/_8$ x 13 $^3/_4$ inches
25.7 x 34.9 centimeters

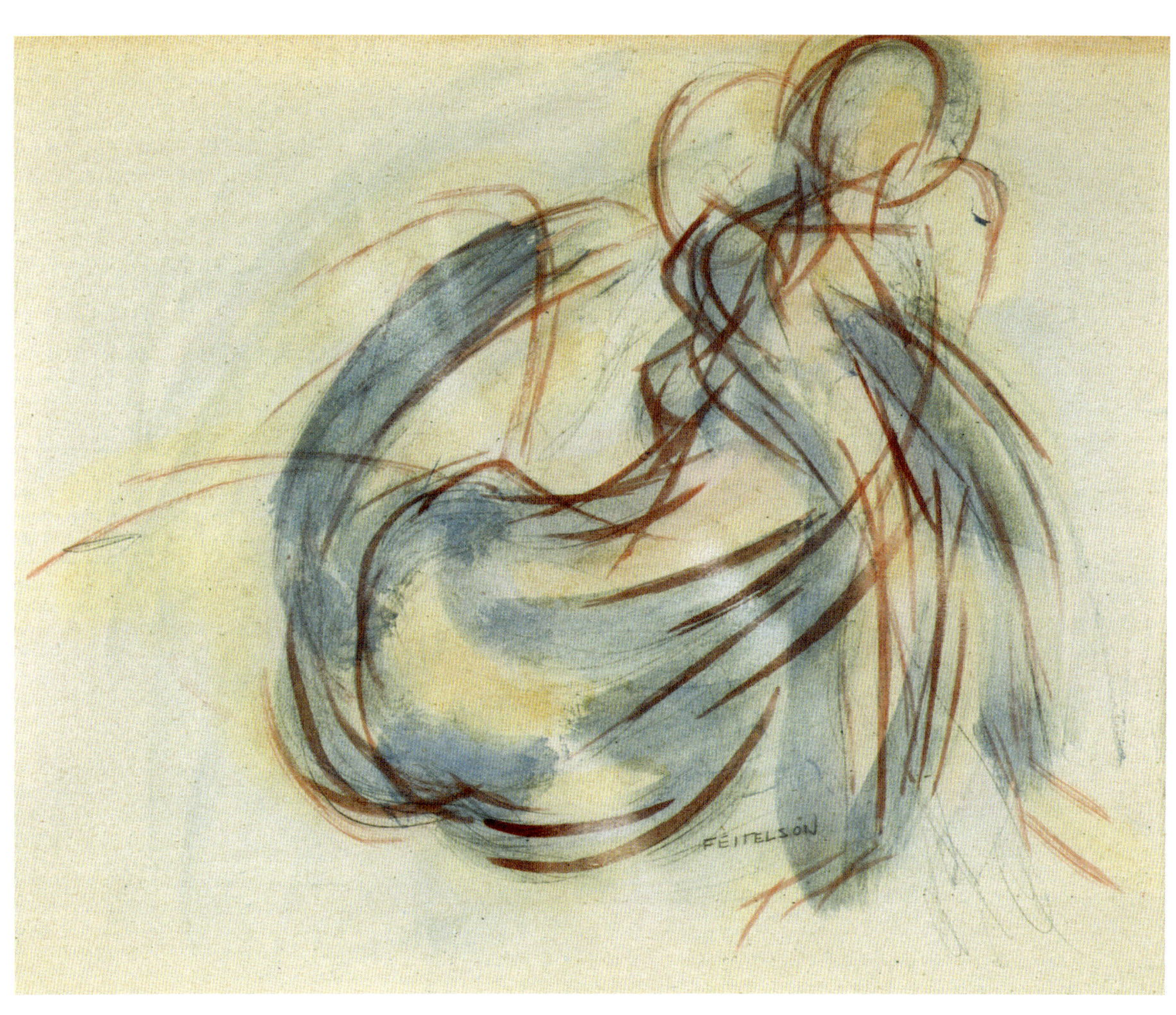
FEITELSON

2.

FIGURE (KINETIC STUDY)

c. 1917-1918
watercolor on carton
4 x 5 1/2 inches
10.2 x 14 centimeters

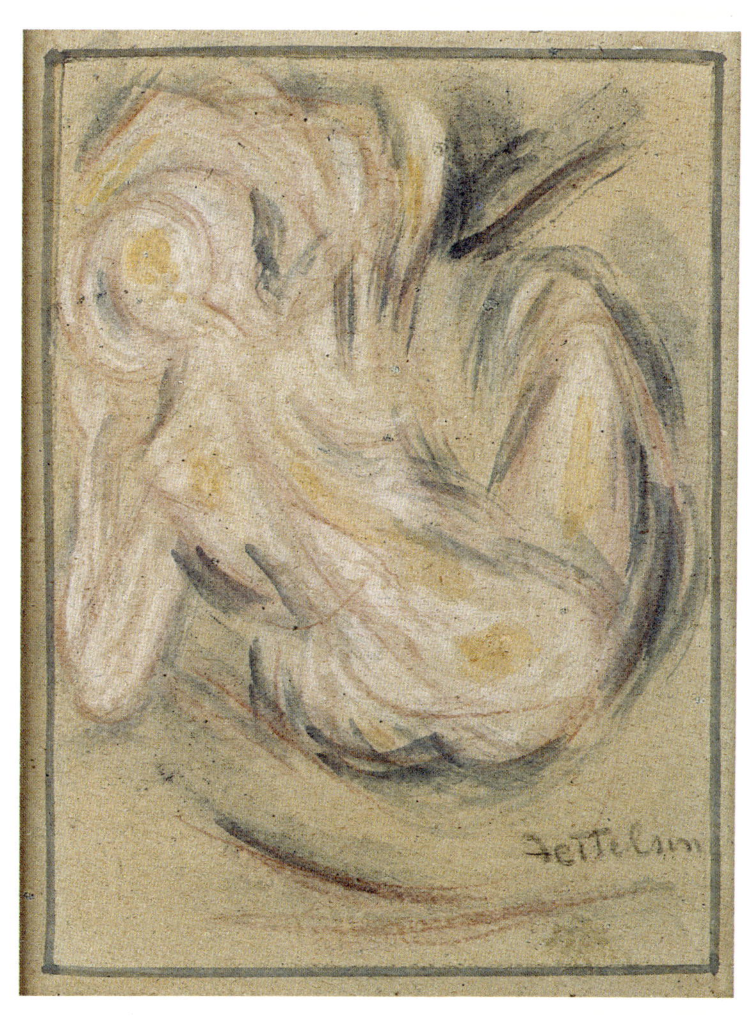

3.

MOTHER AND CHILD
(KINETIC STUDY)

circa 1918
pastel and watercolor on carton
20 x 24 inches
50.8 x 61 centimeters

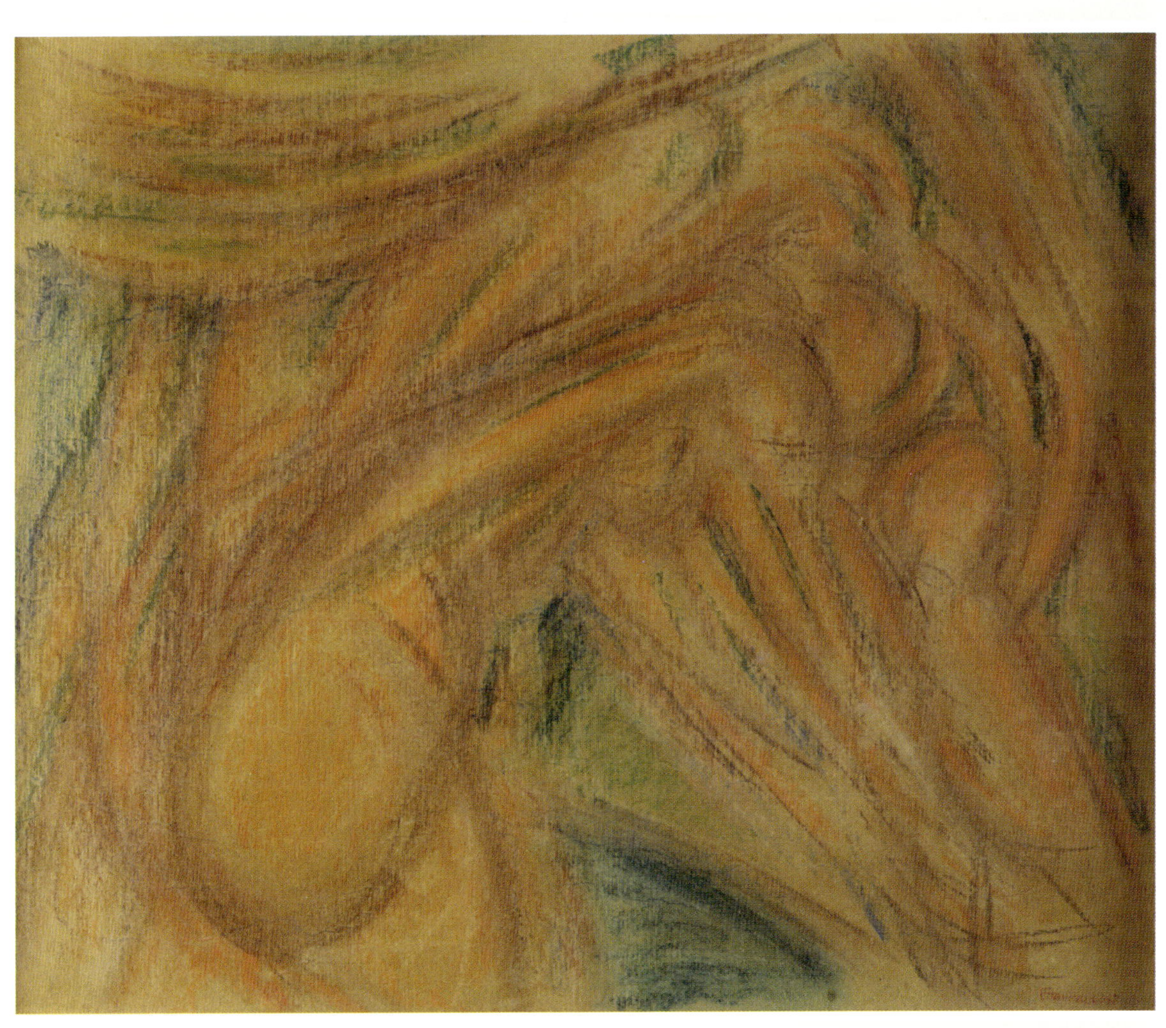

4.

TWO FIGURES

1918-19
oil on carton
9 x 12 inches
22.9 x 30.5 centimeters

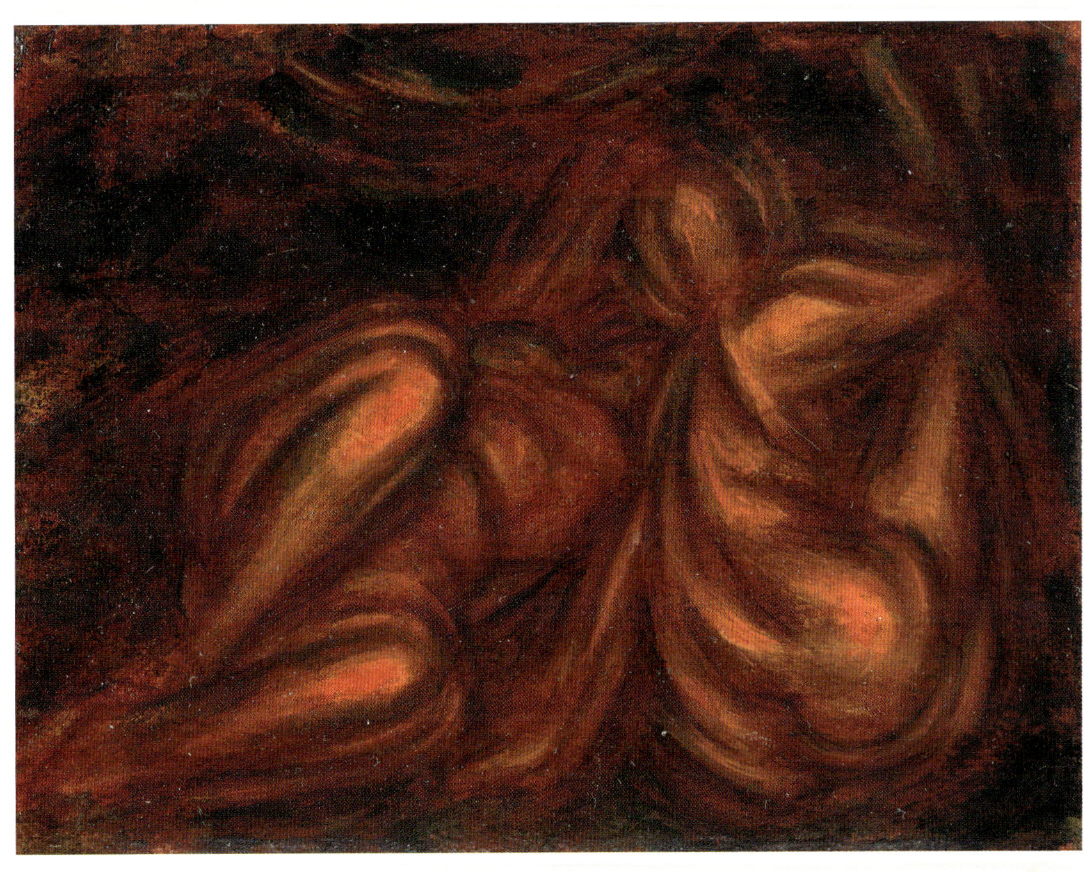

5.

FIGURE GROUP
(STUDY IN KINETICS)

1918-19
oil on carton
11 $^1/_2$ x 27 inches
29.2 x 68.6 centimeters

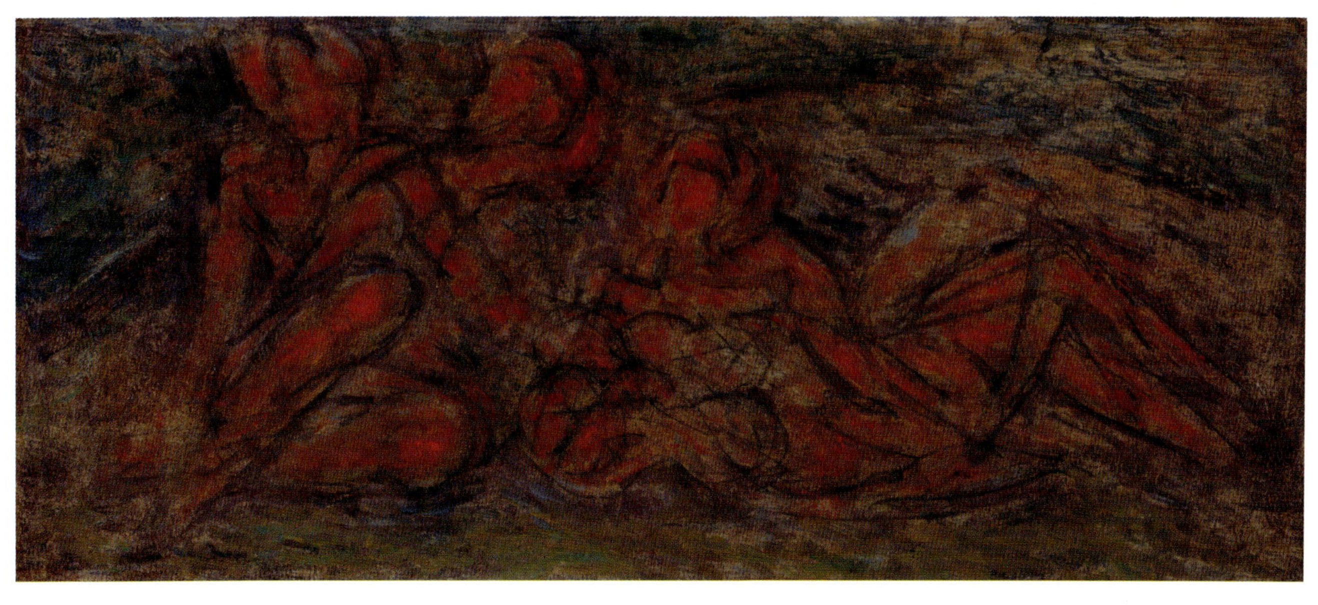

6.

LEDA
(STUDY IN KINETICS)

1918-1919
oil on carton
24 x 26 inches
61 x 66 centimeters

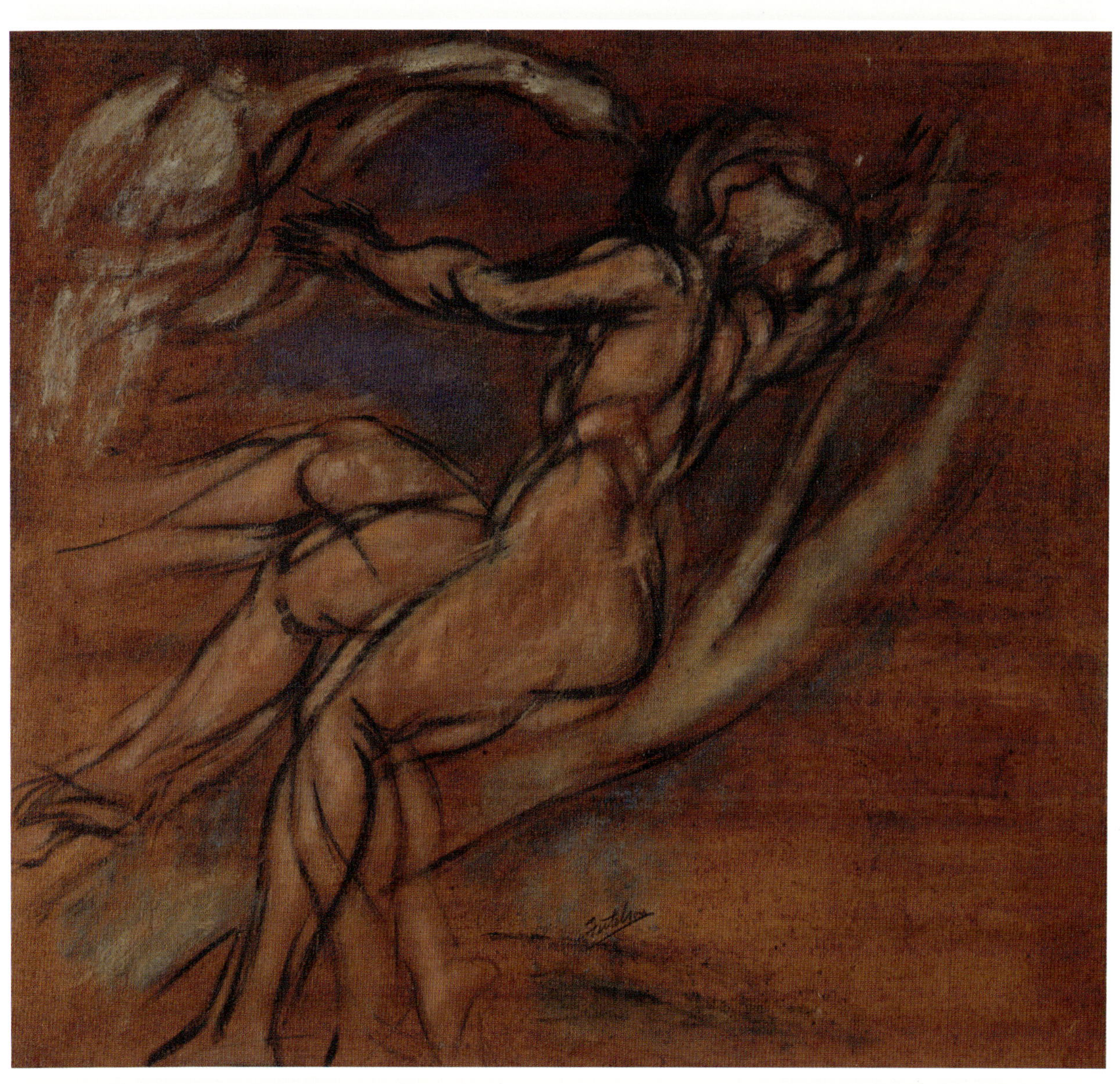

7.

FIGURES

1918-1919
oil on carton
17 1/4 x 17 1/4 inches
43.8 x 43.8 centimeters

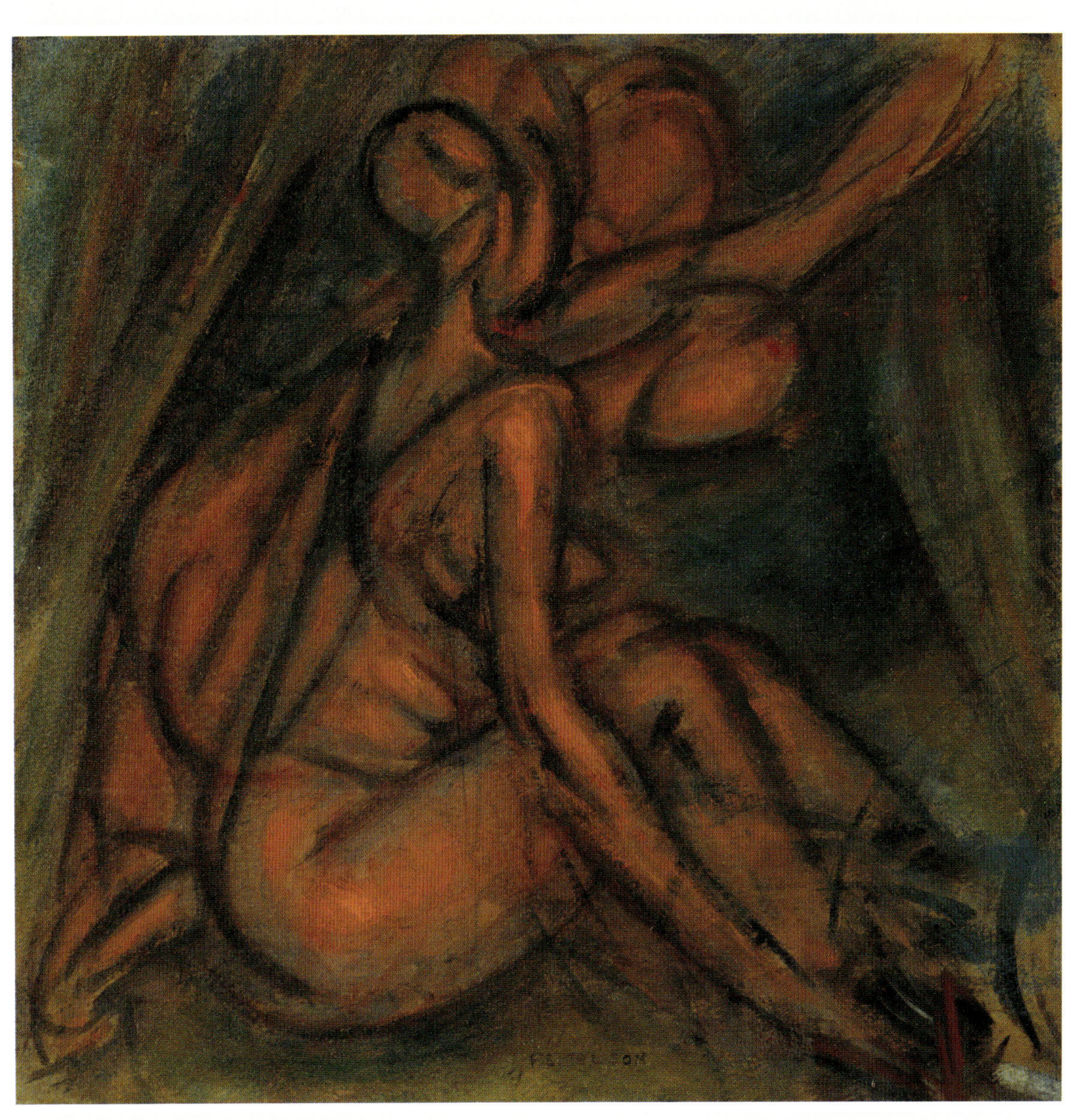

8.

BATHERS #8

1918-1919
oil on carton
16 x 20 inches
40.6 x 50.8 centimeters

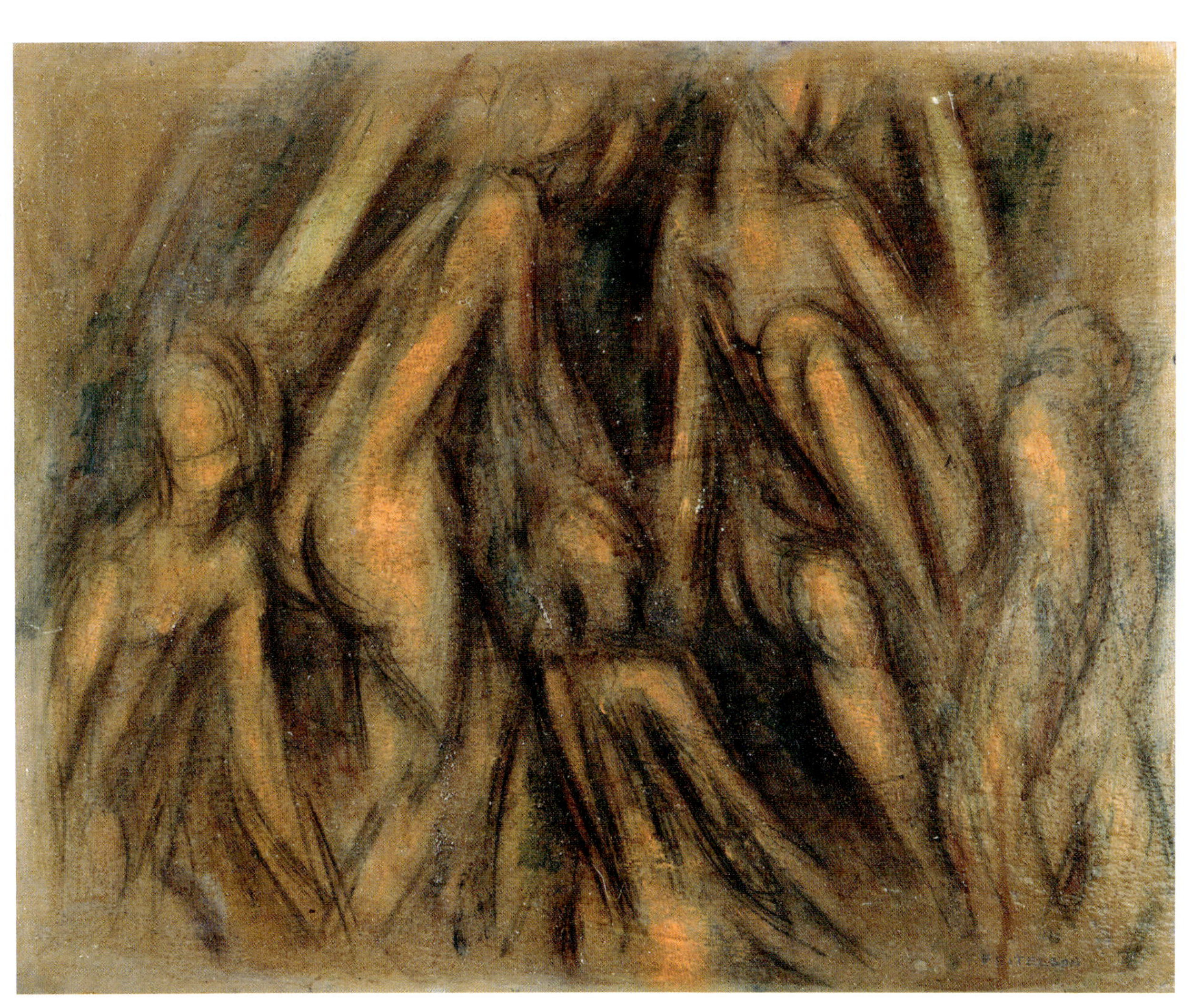

9.

LANDSCAPE WITH TWO FIGURES

1918-1919
watercolor and graphite on paper
9 x 12 inches
22.9 x 30.5 centimeters

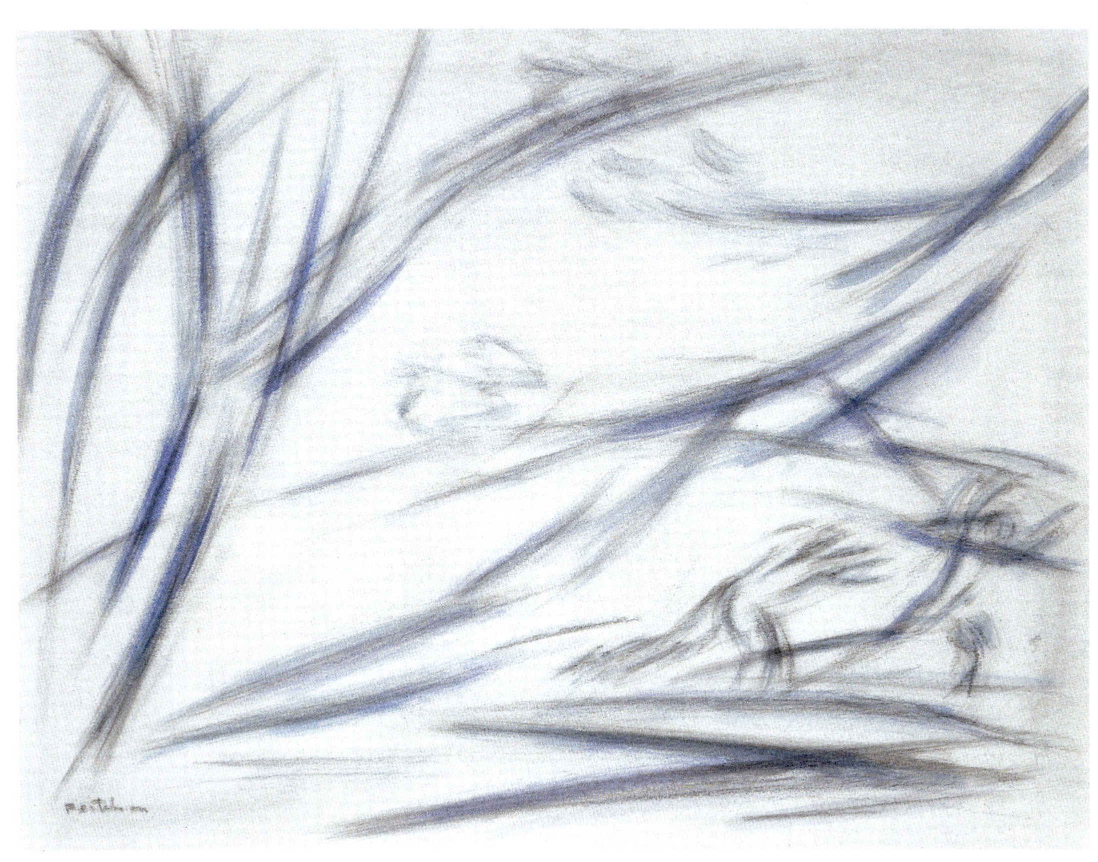

10.

FIGURE

1918-1920
oil on carton
21 x 19 3/4 inches
53.3 x 50.2 centimeters

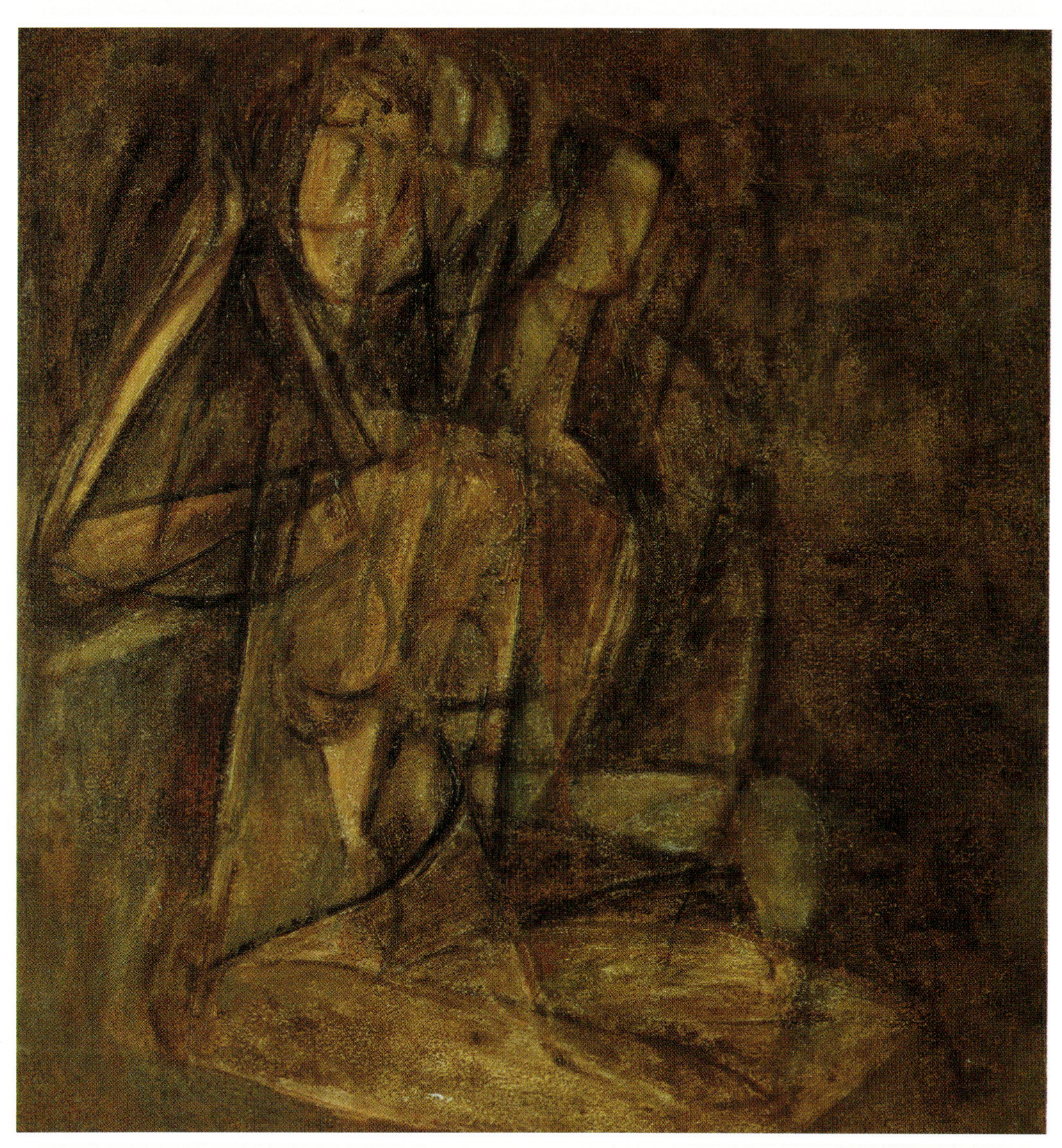

11.

THREE FIGURES

1919
Conte crayon on paper
9 1/4 x 11 1/4 inches
23.5 x 28.6 cm

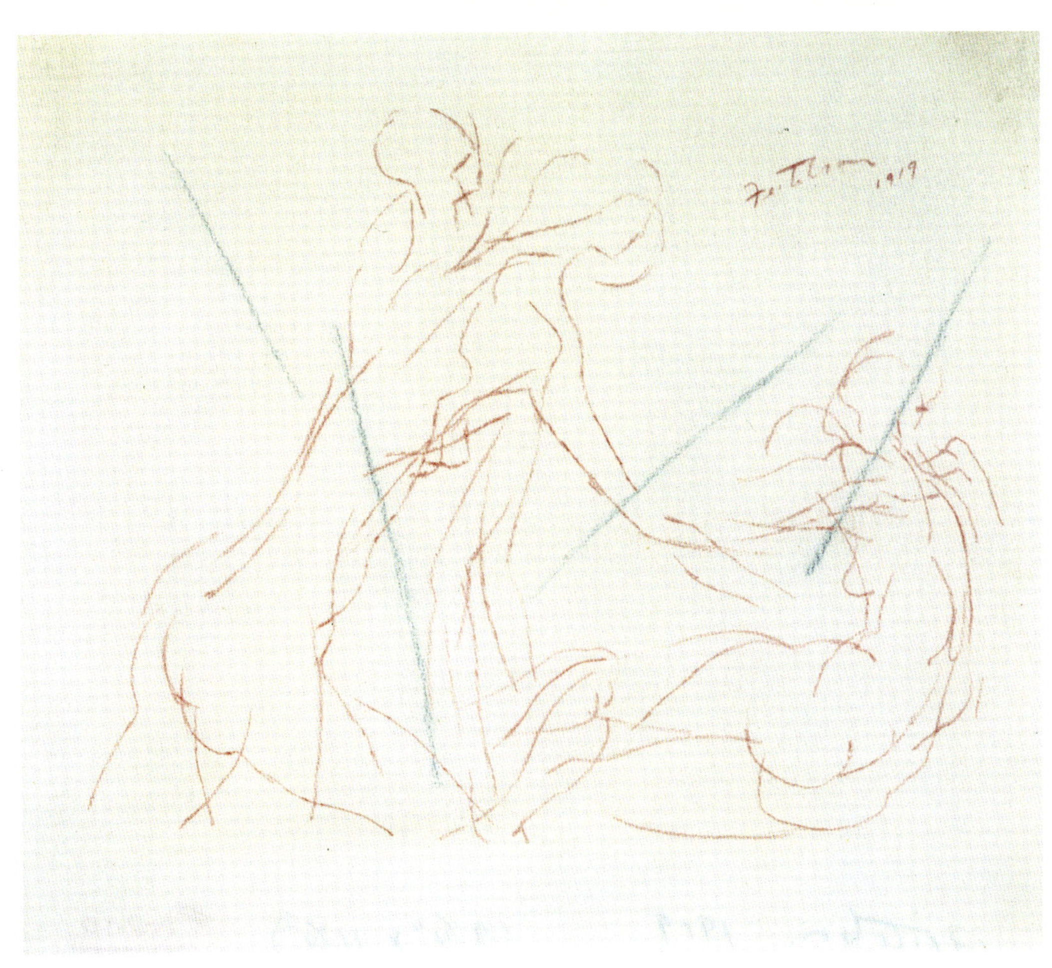
Feininger 1919

12.

TWO NUDES
(MALE AND FEMALE)

1919
Conte crayon on paper
11 1/2 x 16 inches
29.2 x 40.6 centimeters

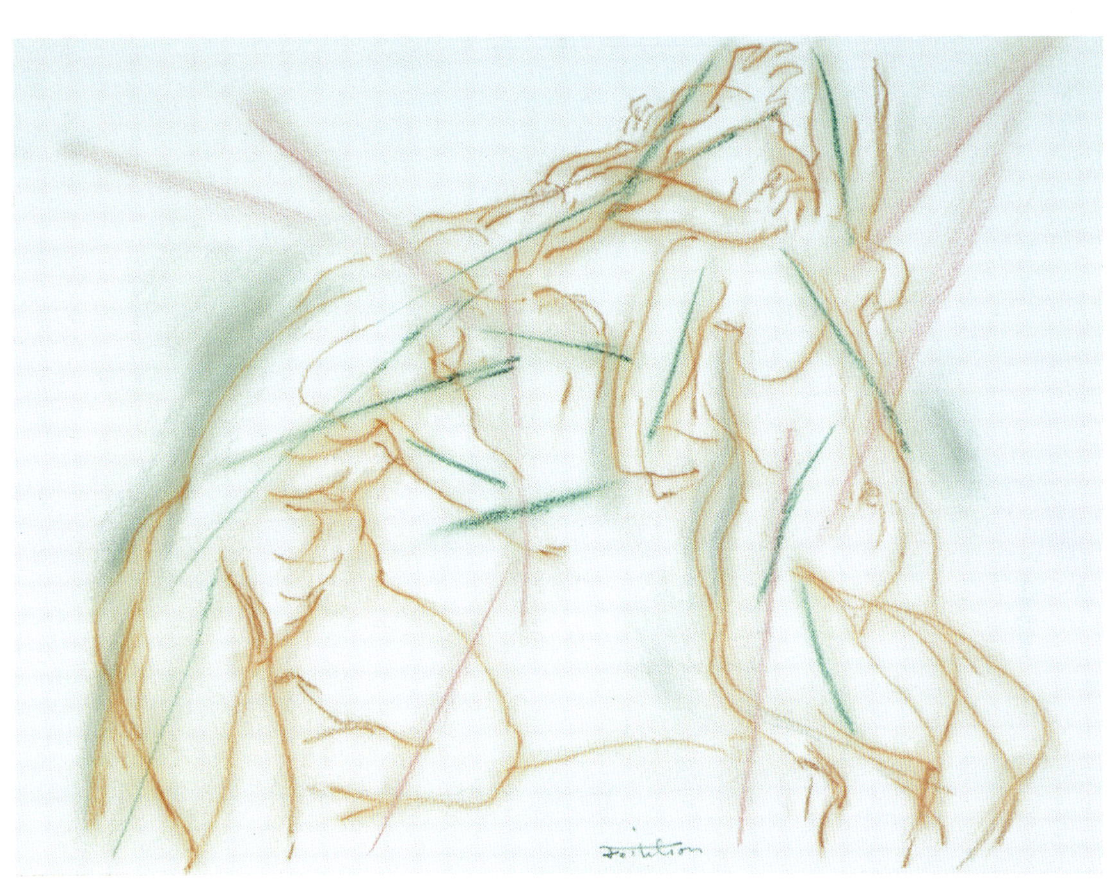

13.

NEW YORK BUILDINGS

1919
Conte crayon, wash and gouache on paper.
11 x 10 inches
27.9 x 25.4 centimeters

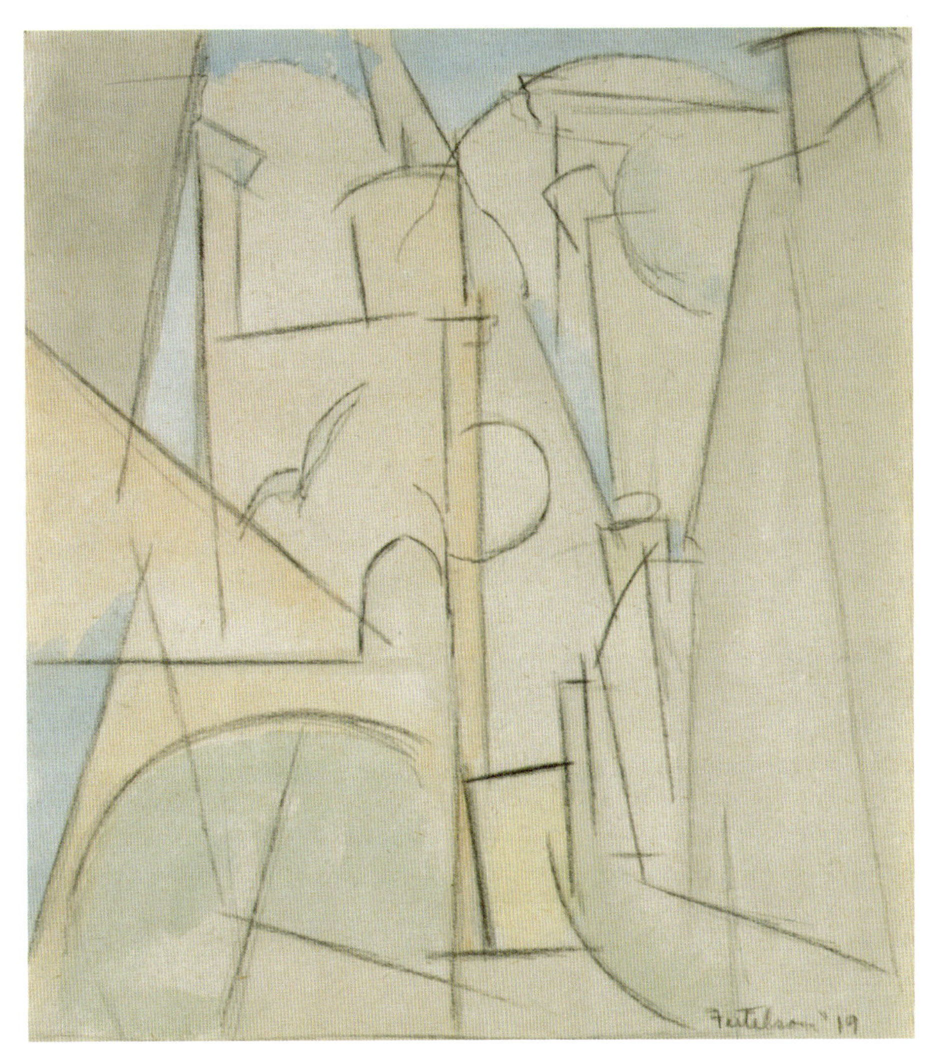

14.

MOTHER AND CHILD

1919
oil on carton
26 x 27 1/2 inches
66 x 69.9 centimeters

15.

TWO NUDES AND A CAT

1919
oil on carton
20 x 24 inches
50.8 x 61 centimeters

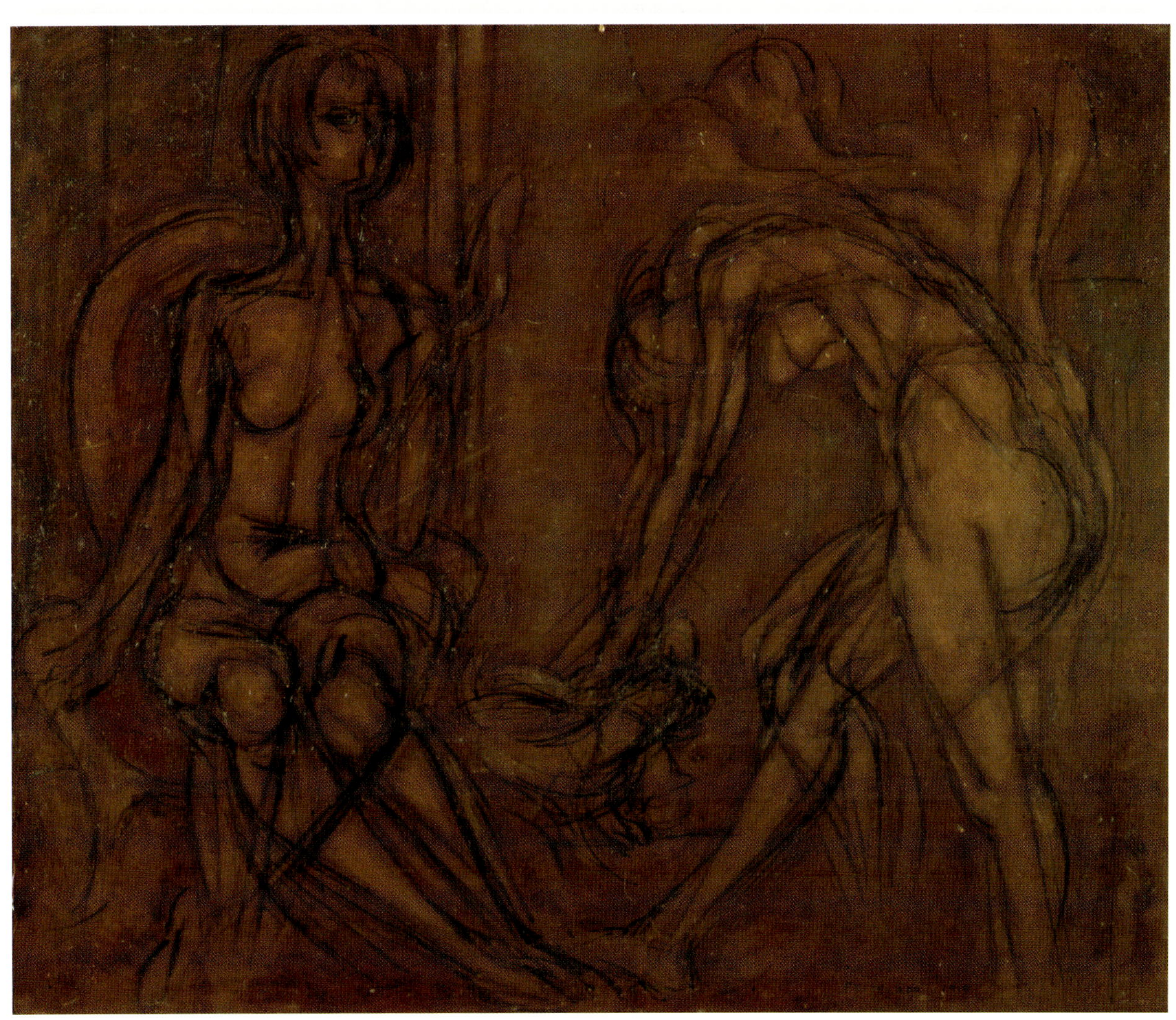

16.

TWO BATHERS
(ORGANIZED ARTICULATION)

1919
oil on carton
23 x 28 inches
58.4 x 71.1 centimeters

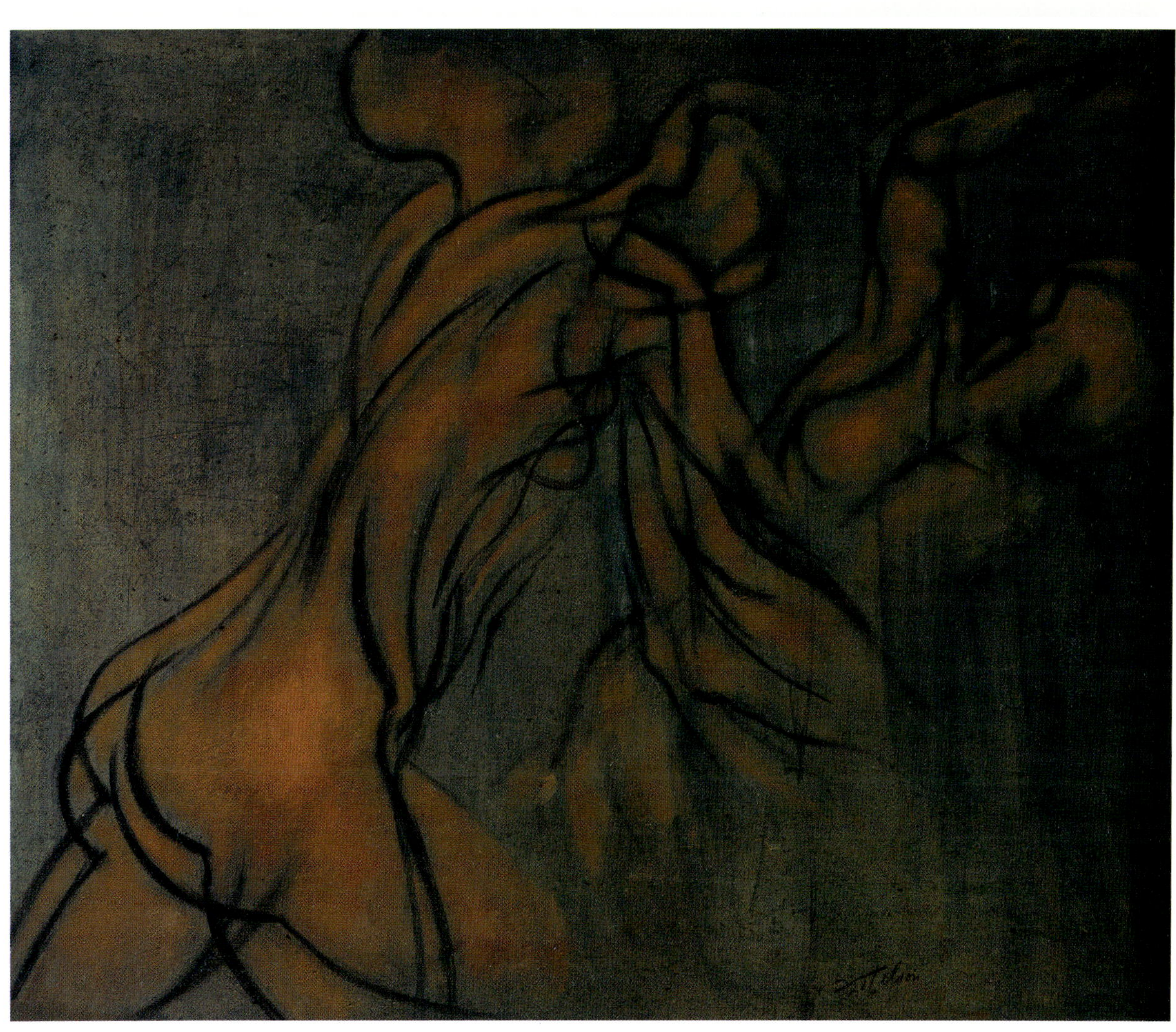

17.

STUDY IN KINETICS

1919
oil on carton
24 1/2 x 19 3/4 inches
62.2 x 50.2 centimeters

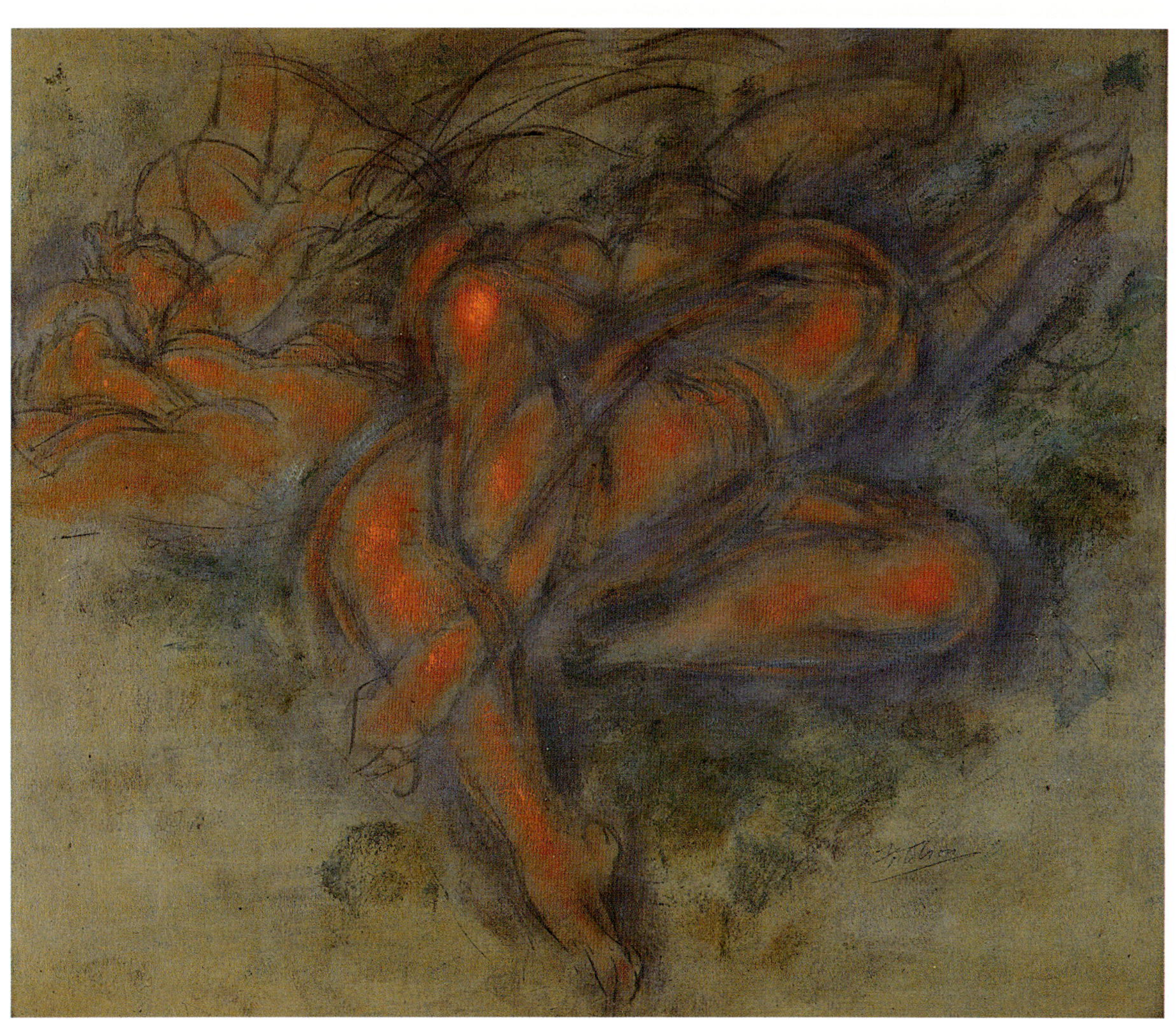

18.

LEDA (STUDY IN KINETICS)

1919
oil on carton
16 x 20 inches
40.6 x 50.8 centimeters

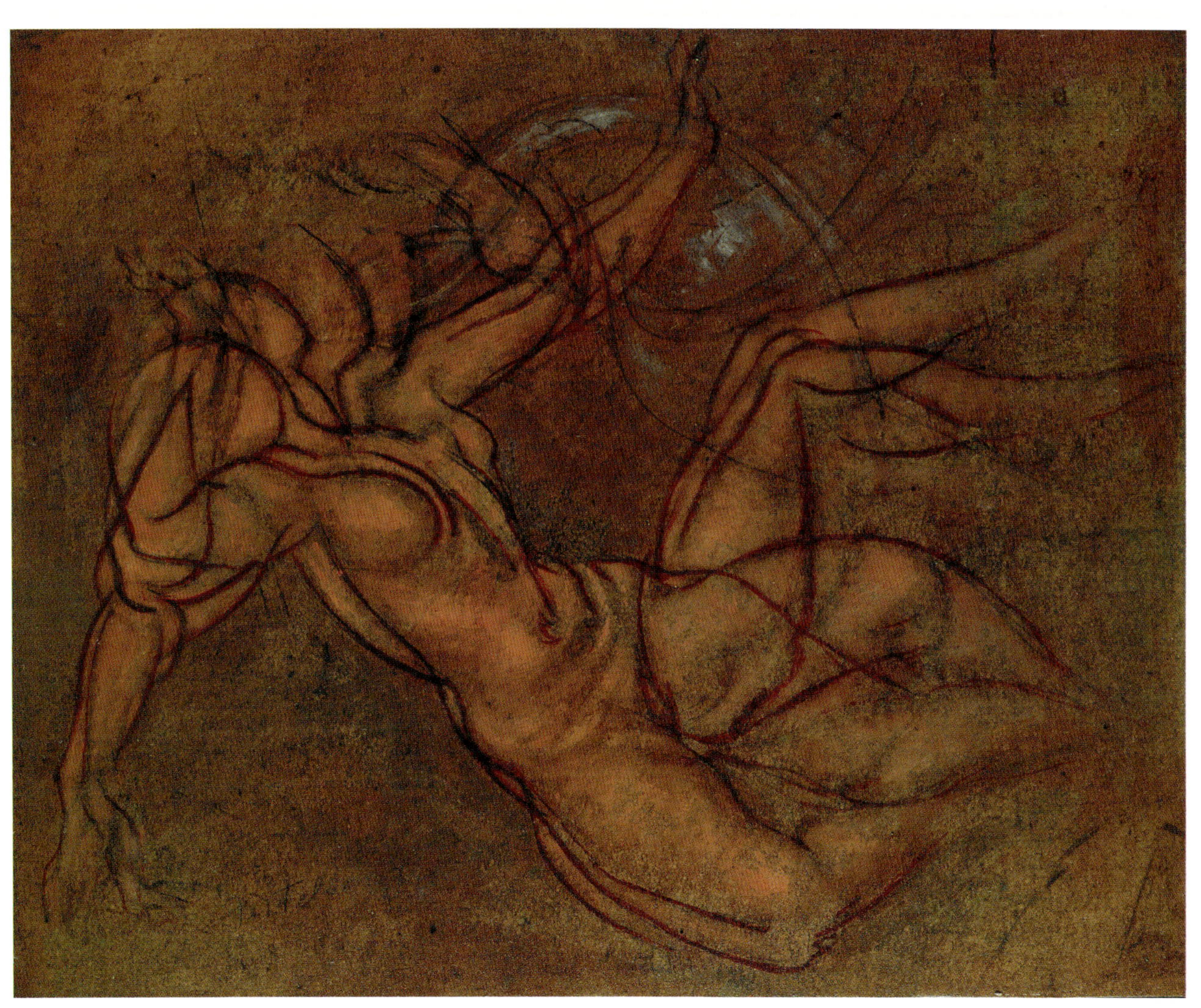

19.

LEDA (STUDY IN KINETICS)

1919
oil on carton
21 $^3/_8$ x 18 $^7/_8$ inches
54.5 x 47.8 centimeters

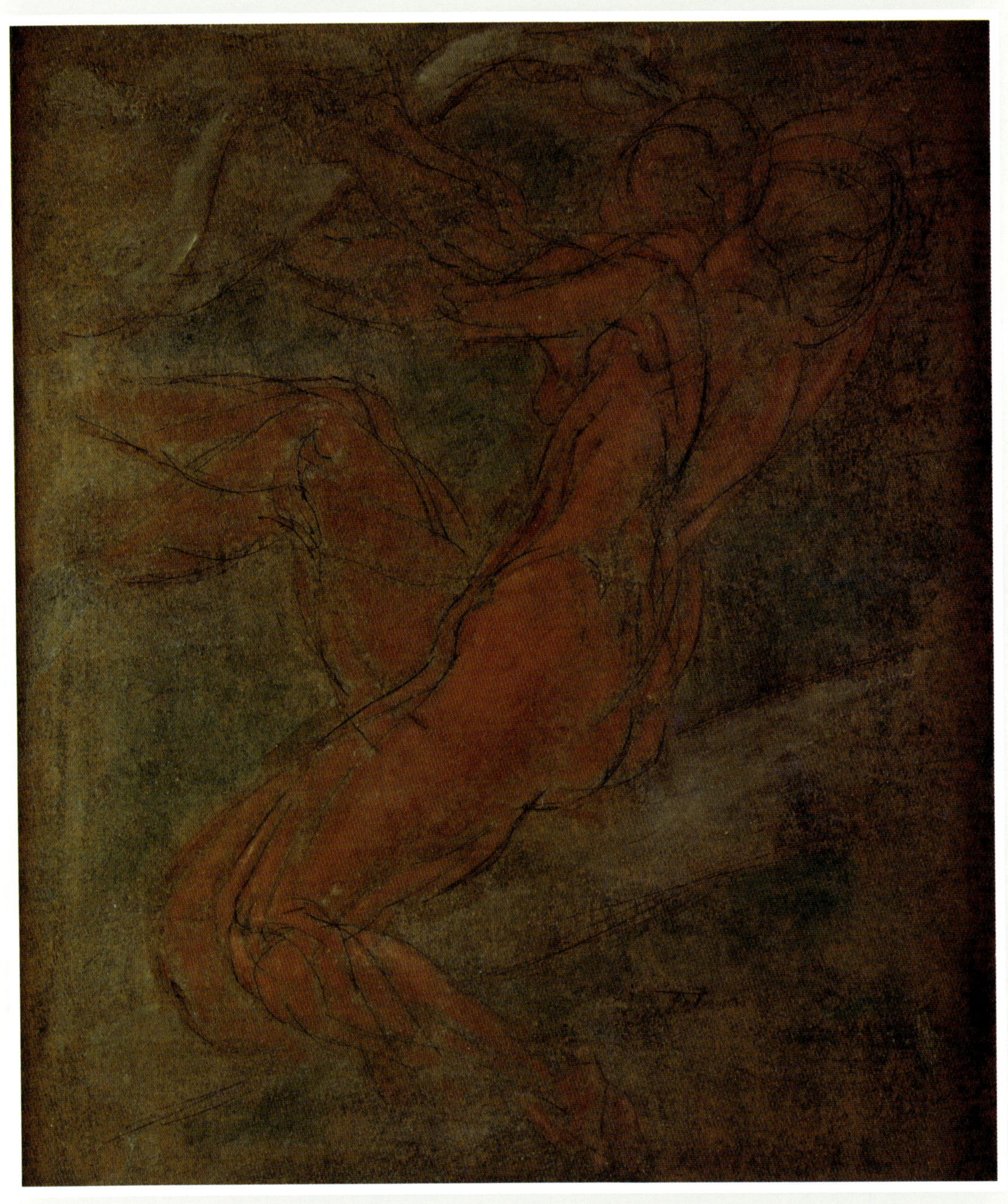

20.

SEATED FEMALE FIGURE
(KINETIC STUDY)

1919
Conte crayon on paper
11 x 13 inches
27.9 x 33 centimeters

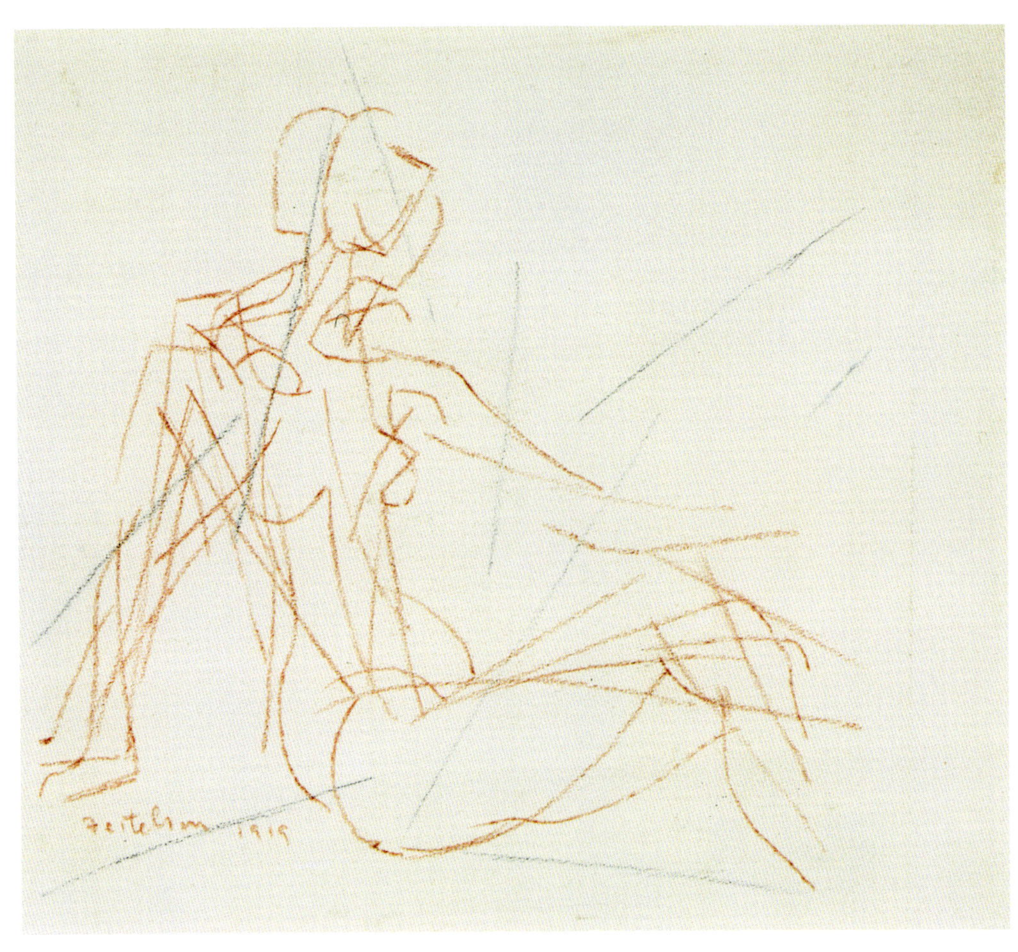

Zeitlin 1919

21.

STUDY FOR LEDA
(STUDY IN KINETICS)

1919
graphite on paper
9 x 12 inches
22.9 x 30.5 centimeters

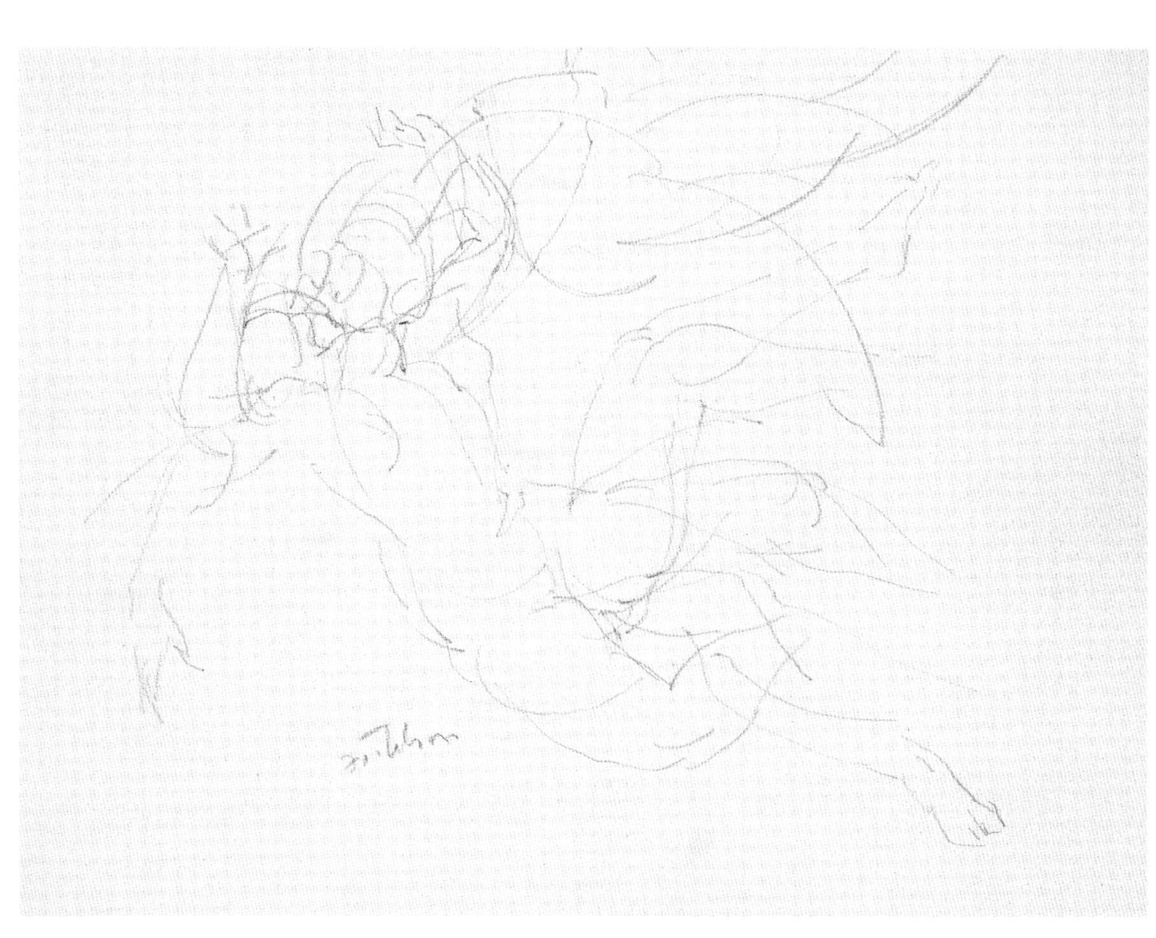

22.

LEDA (STUDY IN KINETICS)

1919
graphite on paper
9 x 12 inches
22.9 x 30.5 centimeters

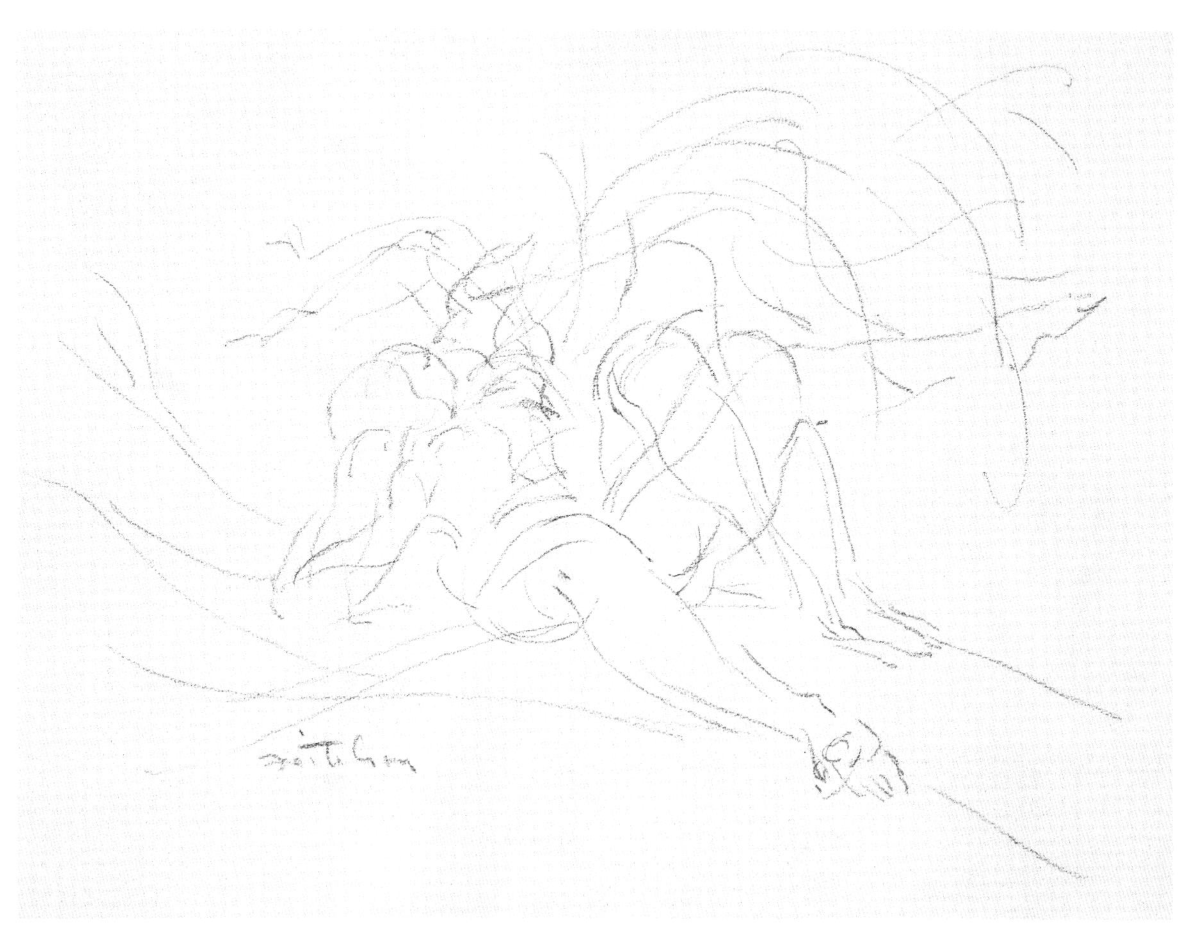

23.

FIGURE (KINETIC ORGANIZATION)

1919-20
oil on carton
28 $^{1}/_{2}$ x 22 $^{3}/_{4}$ inches
72.4 x 57.8 centimeters

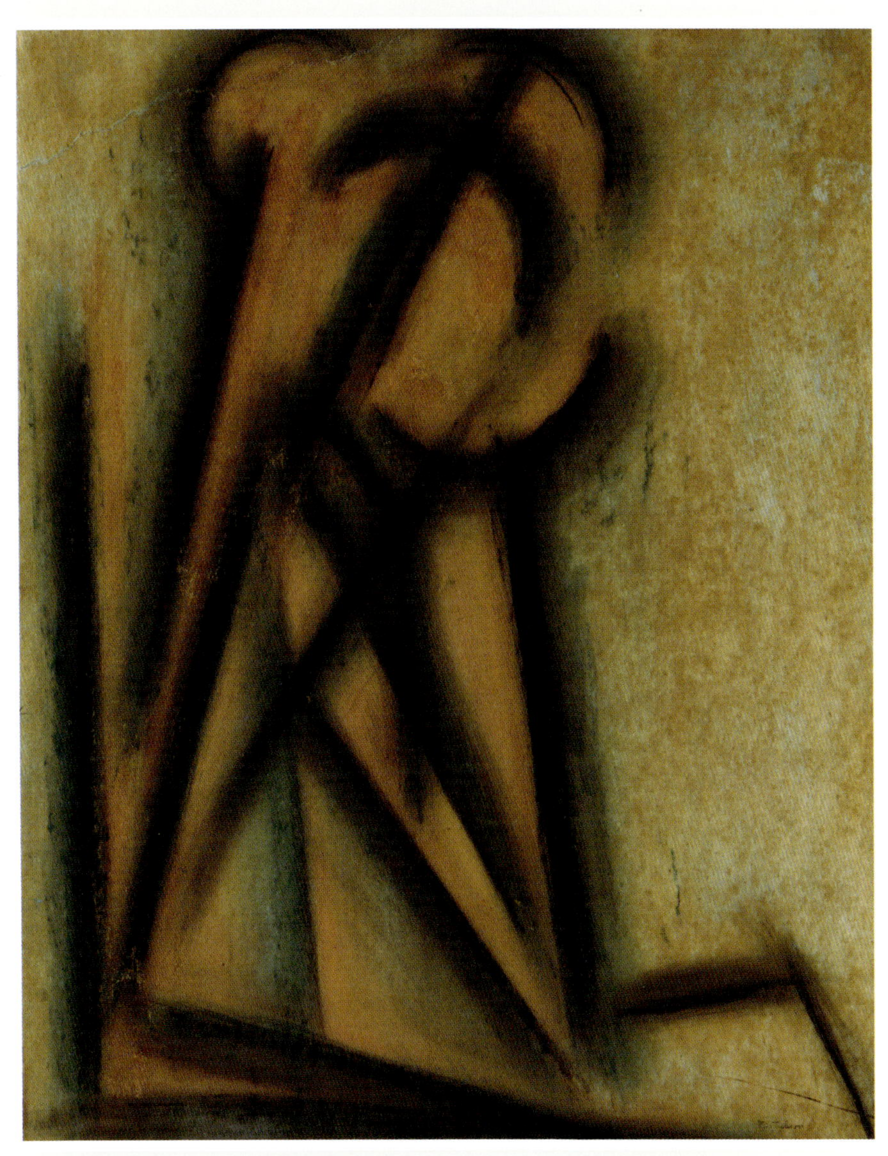

24.

KINETIC FIGURE

1919-20
oil on carton
30 x 24 inches
76.2 x 61 centimeters

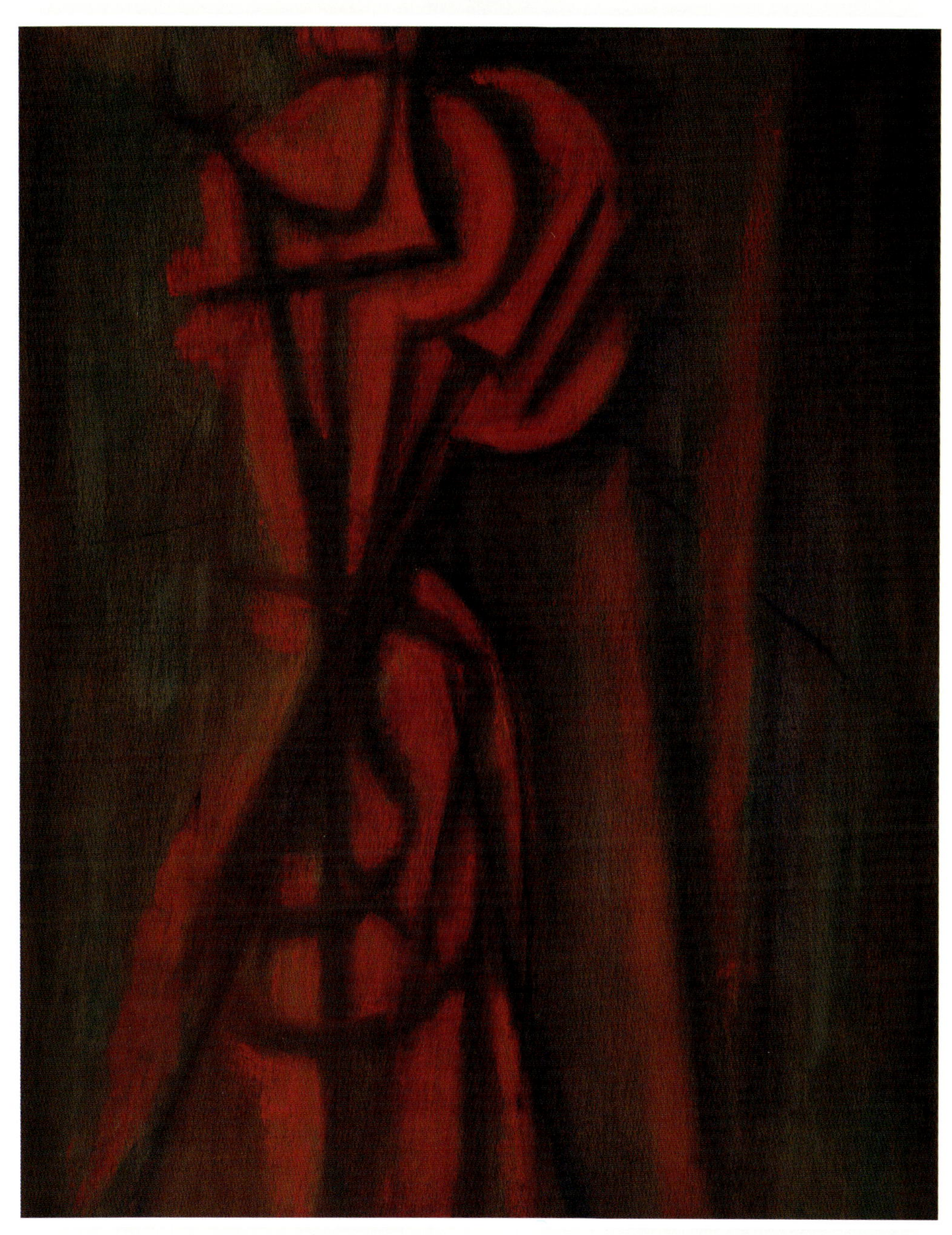

25.

TWO BATHERS
(KINETIC STUDY)

1919-20
Oil on carton
20 x 16 inches
50.8 x 40.6 centimeters

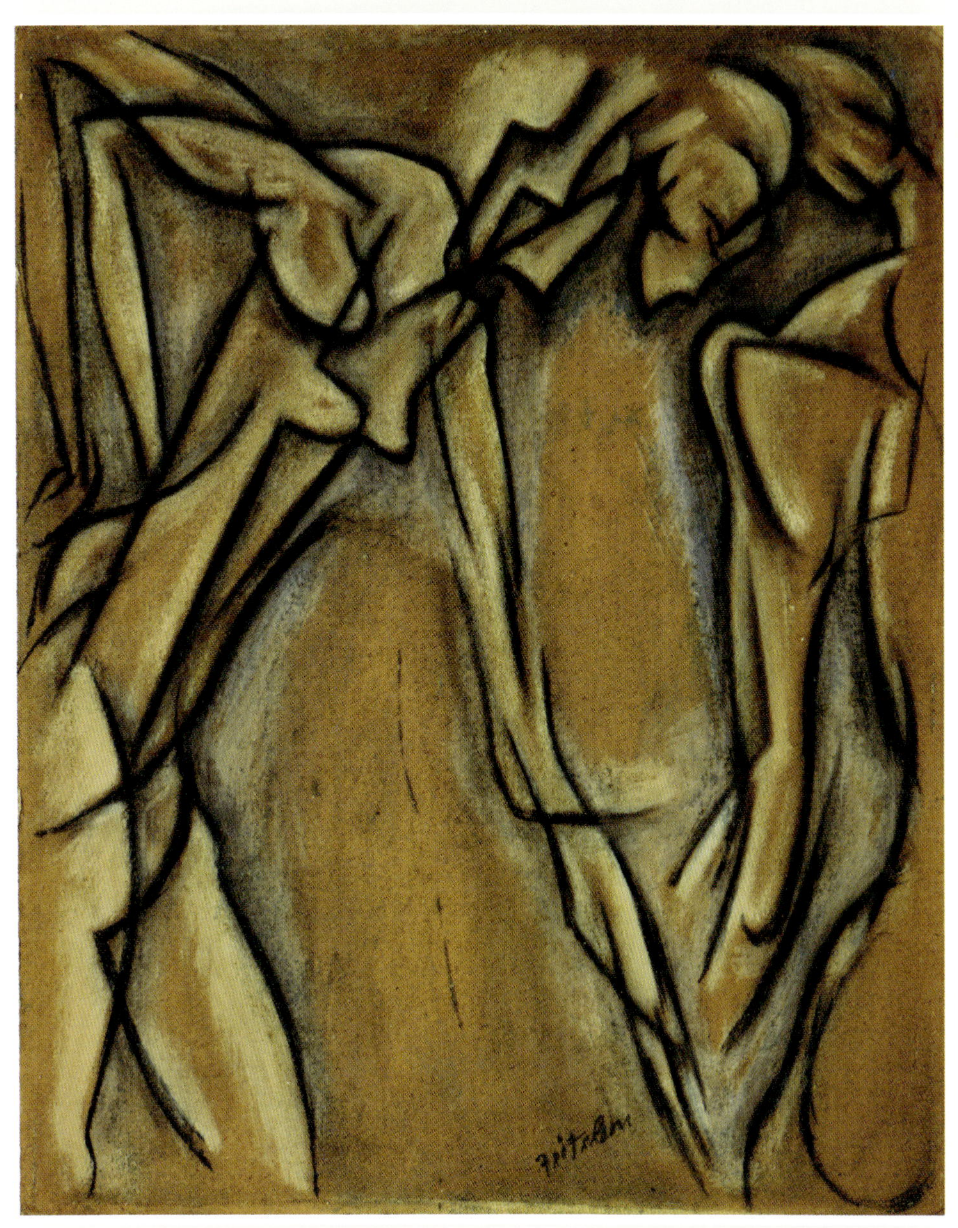

26.

TWO BATHERS
(KINETIC ORGANIZATION)

1919-20
oil on carton
29 x 22 $^3/_4$ inches
73.7 x 57.8 centimeters

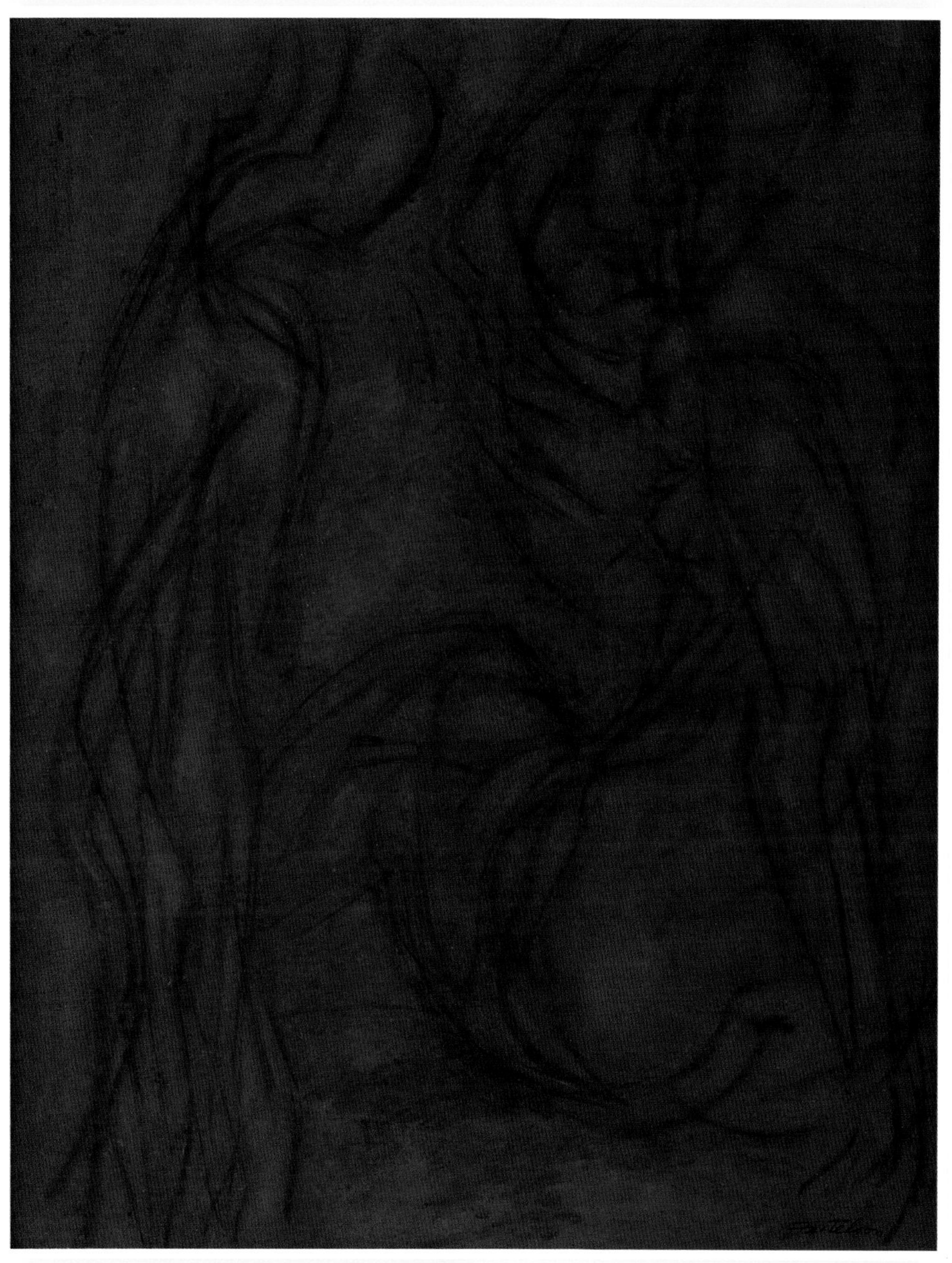

27.

MOTHER AND CHILD
(BATHERS, KINETIC ORGANIZATION)

1919-1920
Oil on carton
12 x 14 inches
30.5 x 35.6 centimeters

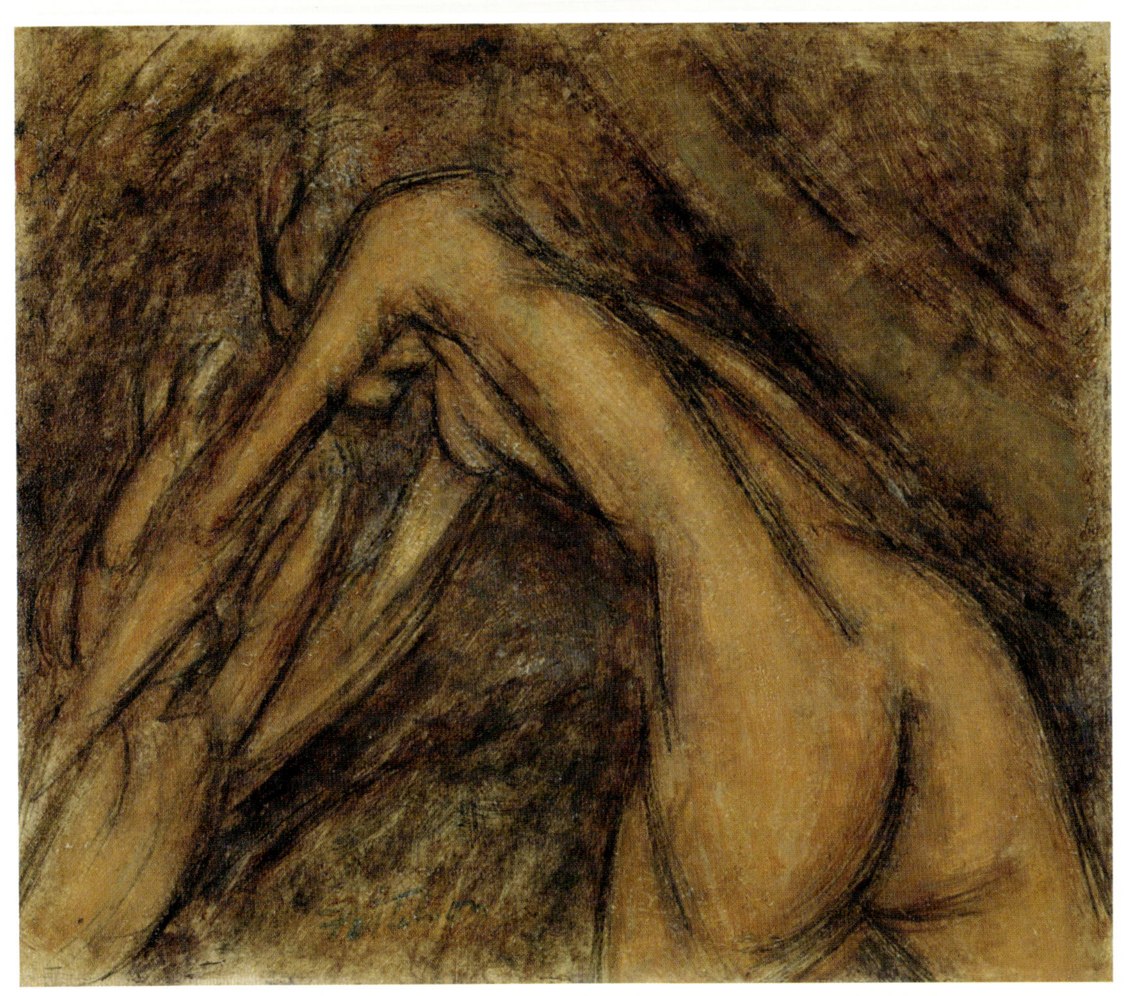

28.

TWO BATHERS
(KINETIC STUDY)

1919-1920
oil on carton
18 $^{1}/_{2}$ x 13 $^{1}/_{4}$ inches
47 x 33.7 centimeters

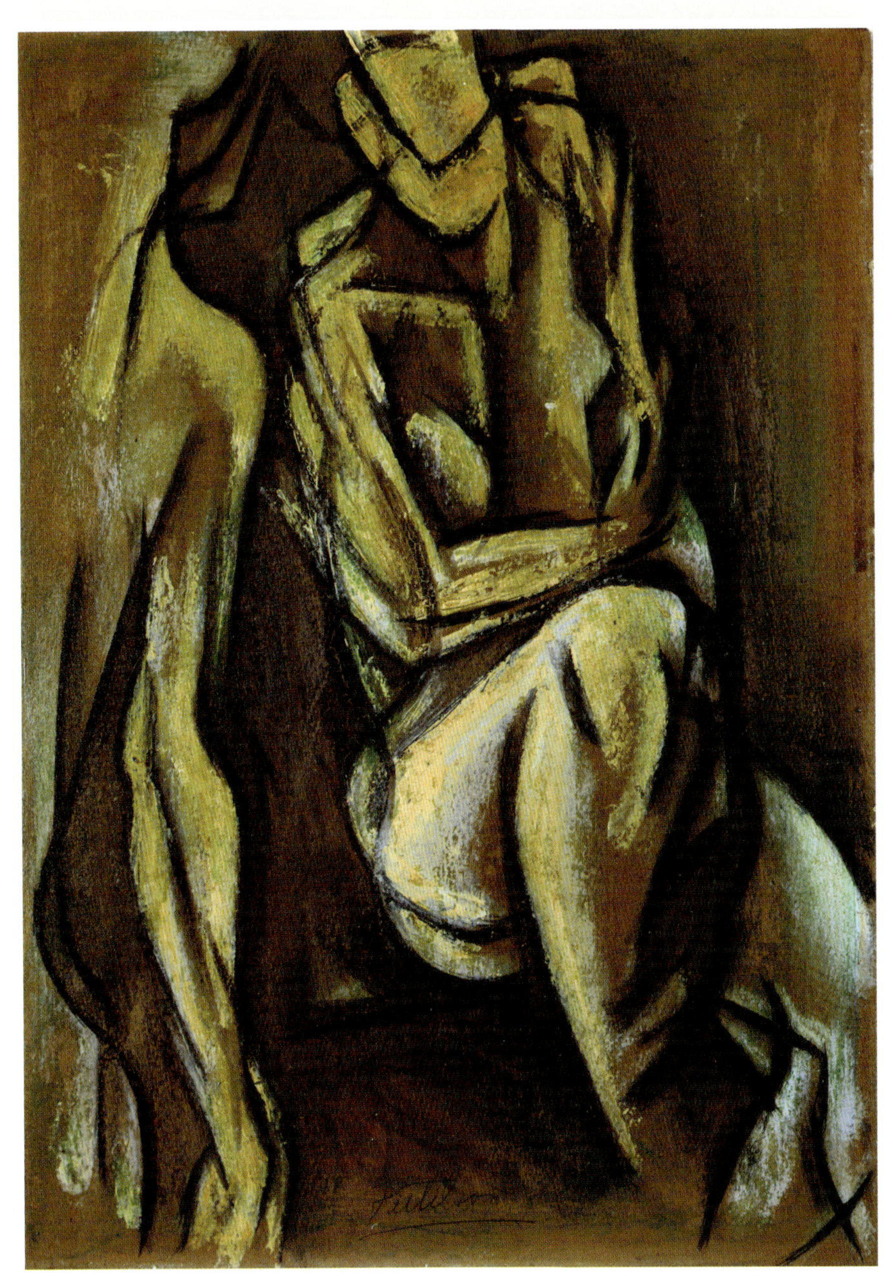

29.

ARCHITECTURAL
ABSTRACTION-BUILDINGS

1920
watercolor and pencil on paper
14 x 11 inches
35.6 x 27.9 centimeters

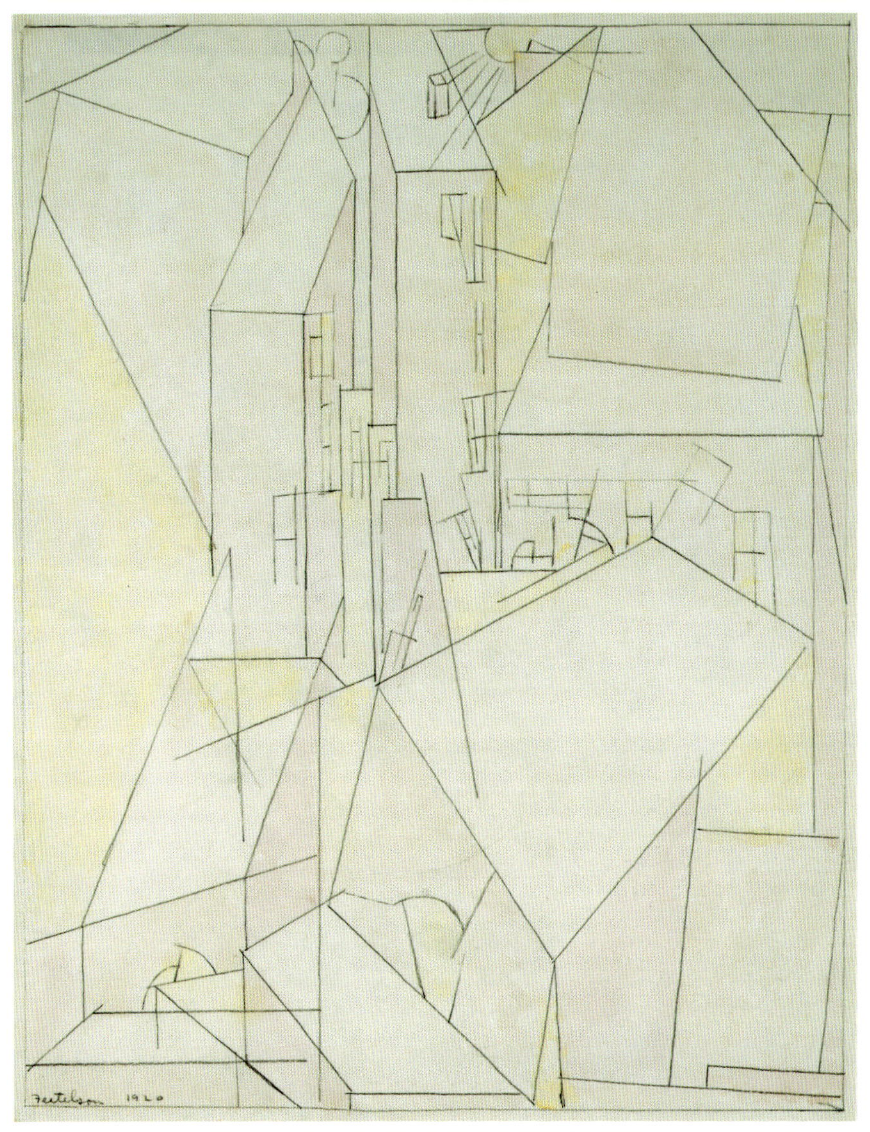

30.

FEMALE FIGURE SEATED AT TABLE

circa 1920
Pencil and watercolor on carton
11 x 8 inches
27.9 x 20.3 centimeters

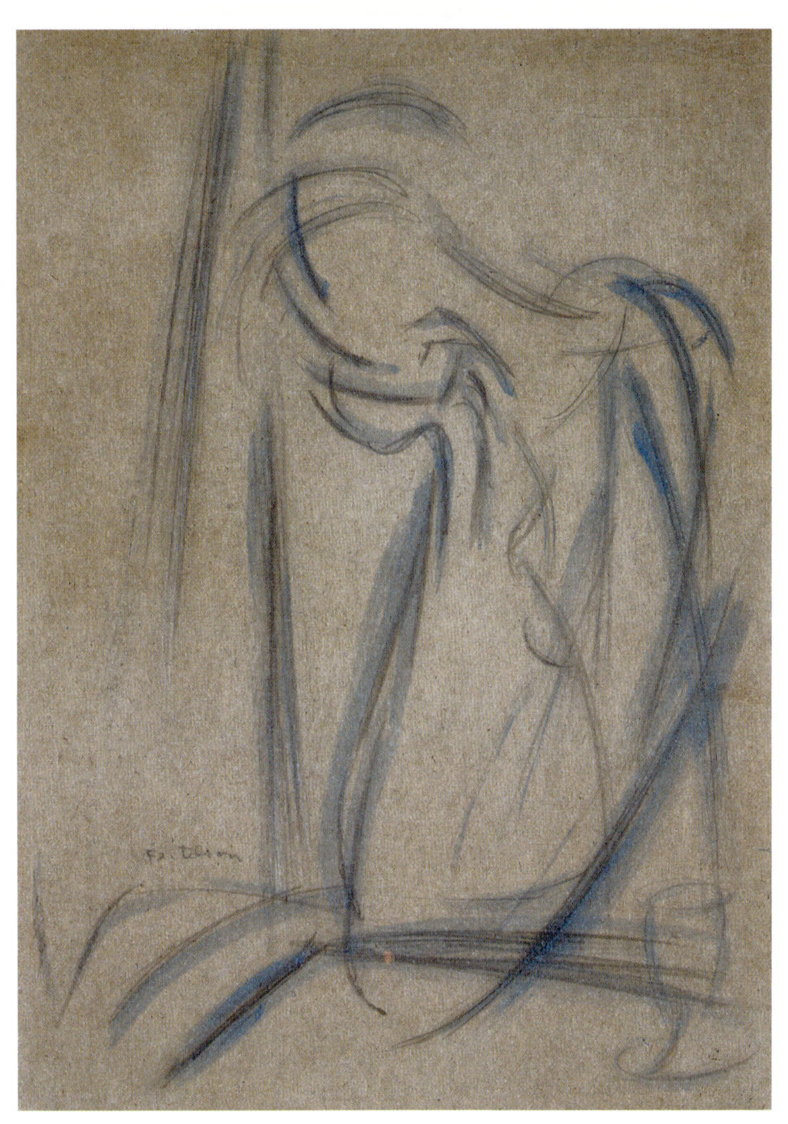

31.

STILL LIFE (2 PEARS, APPLE)

circa 1920
charcoal and oil pastel on paper
8 1/2 x 11 1/2 inches
21.6 x 29.2 centimeters

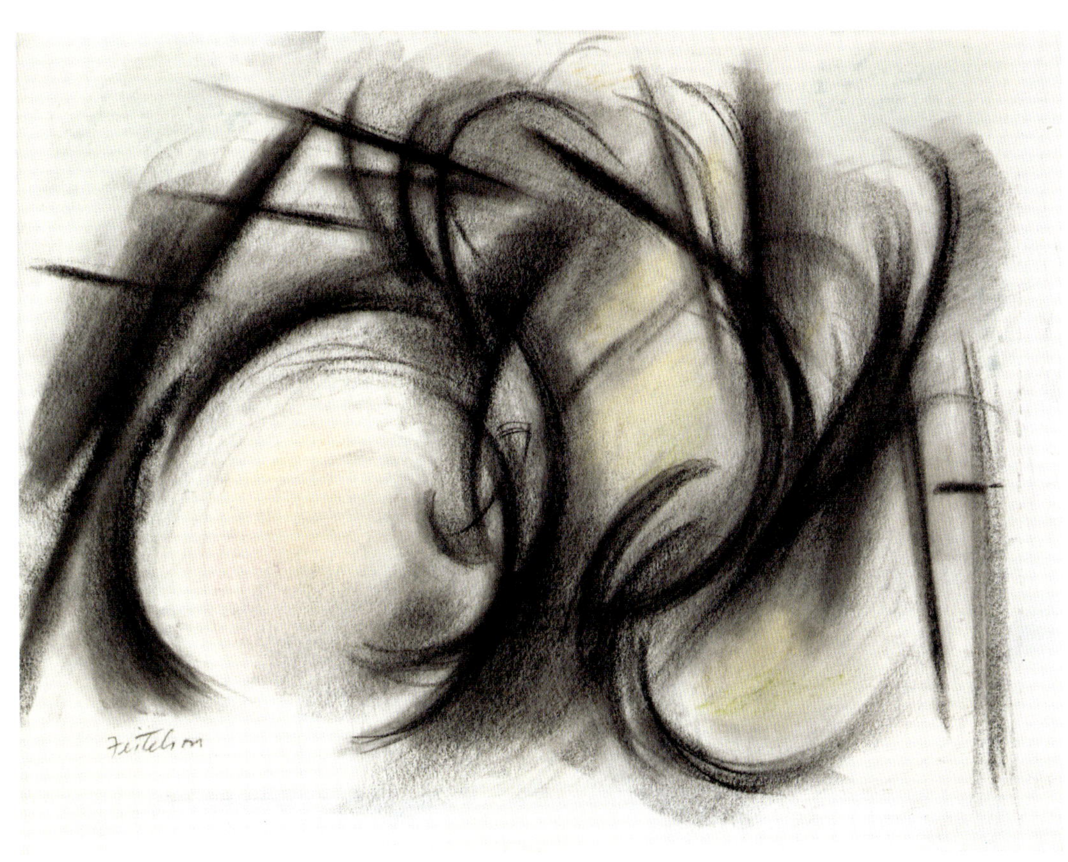

32.

STILL LIFE (2 APPLES, PEAR)

circa 1920
charcoal and oil pastel on paper
8 1/2 x 11 1/2 inches
21.6 x 29.2 centimeters

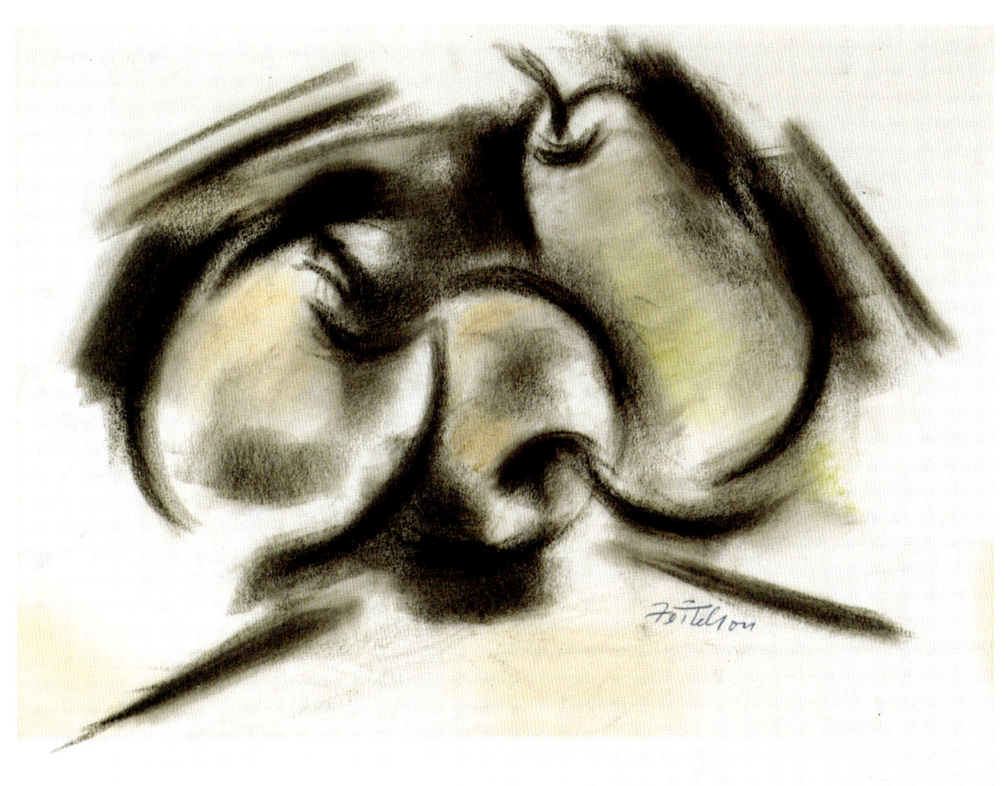

33.

PEARS AND APPLES

1920
oil on board
9 x 12 inches
30.5 x 22.9 centimeters

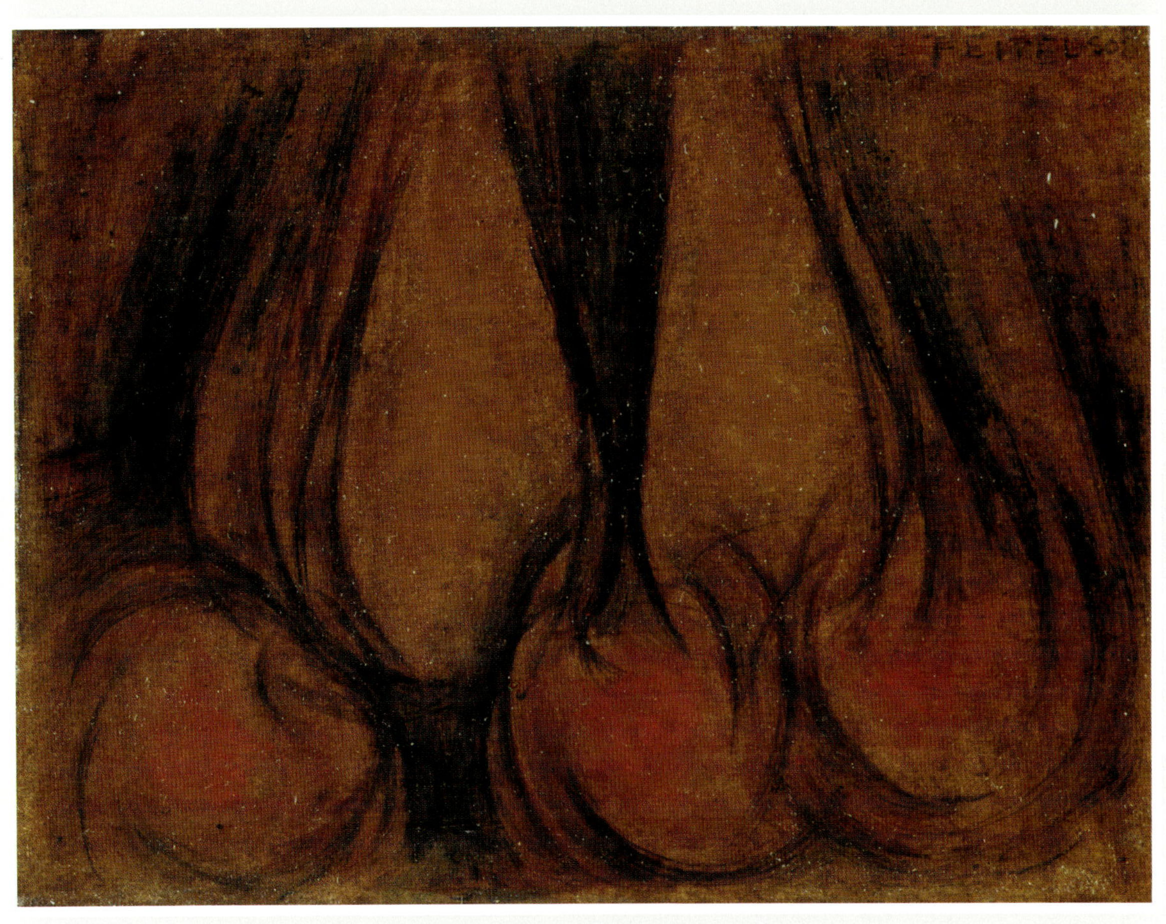

34.

INTERIOR

1921
Conte crayon on paper
21 x 17 ¹/4 inches
53.3 x 43.8 centimeters

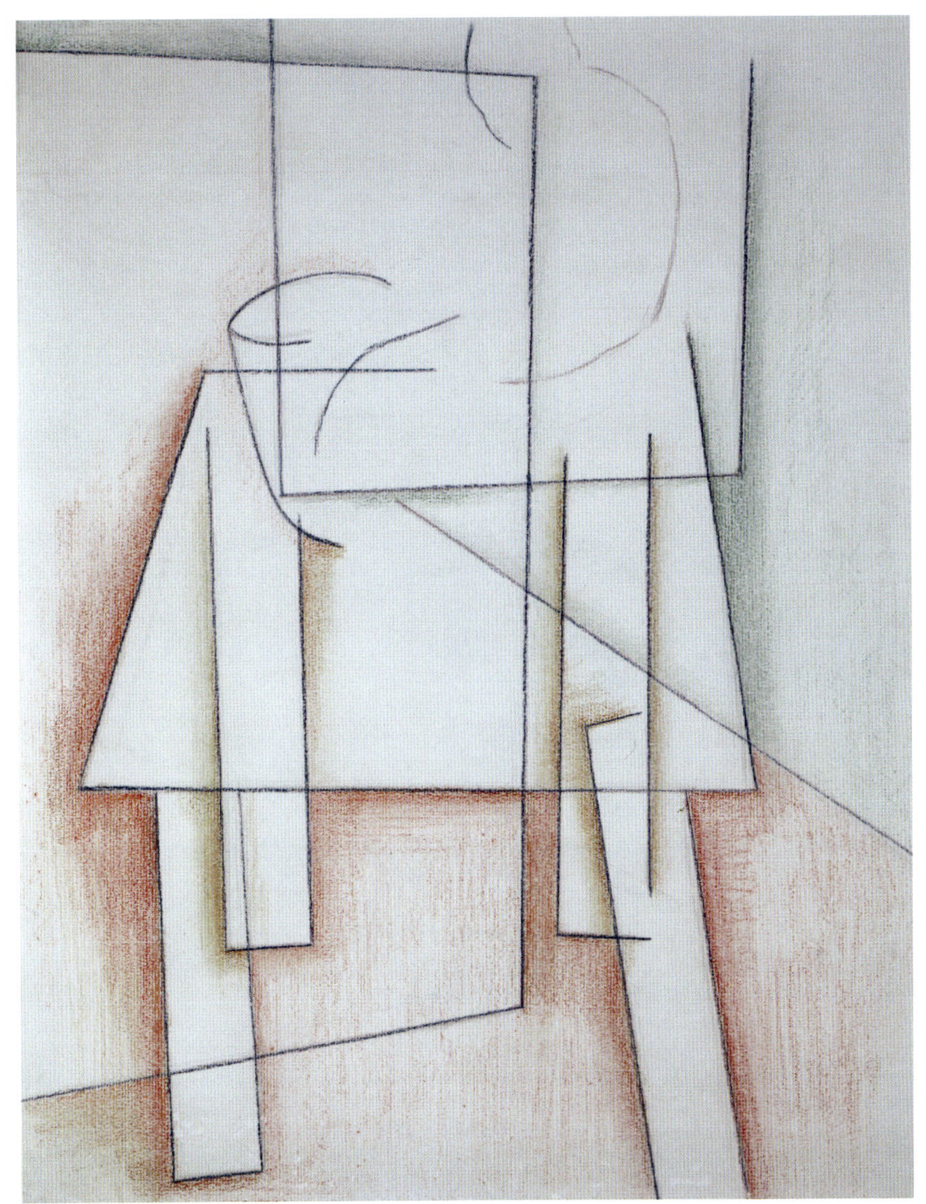

35.

FEMALE FIGURE

1921
oil pastel and Conte crayon on paper
10 $^3/_8$ x 6 inches
26.4 x 15.2 centimeters

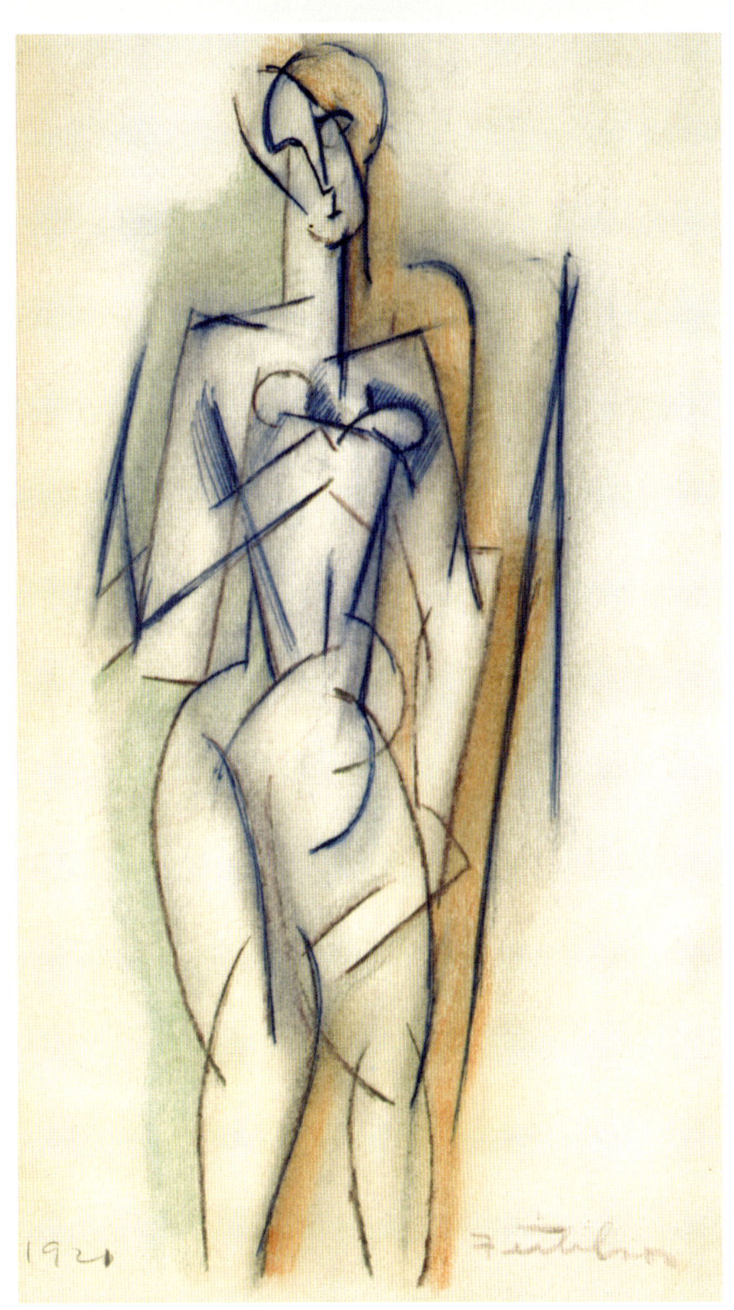
1920

36.

BATHERS
(KINETIC COMPOSITION)

before 1923
oil on carton
20 x 24 inches
50.4 x 59.7 centimeters

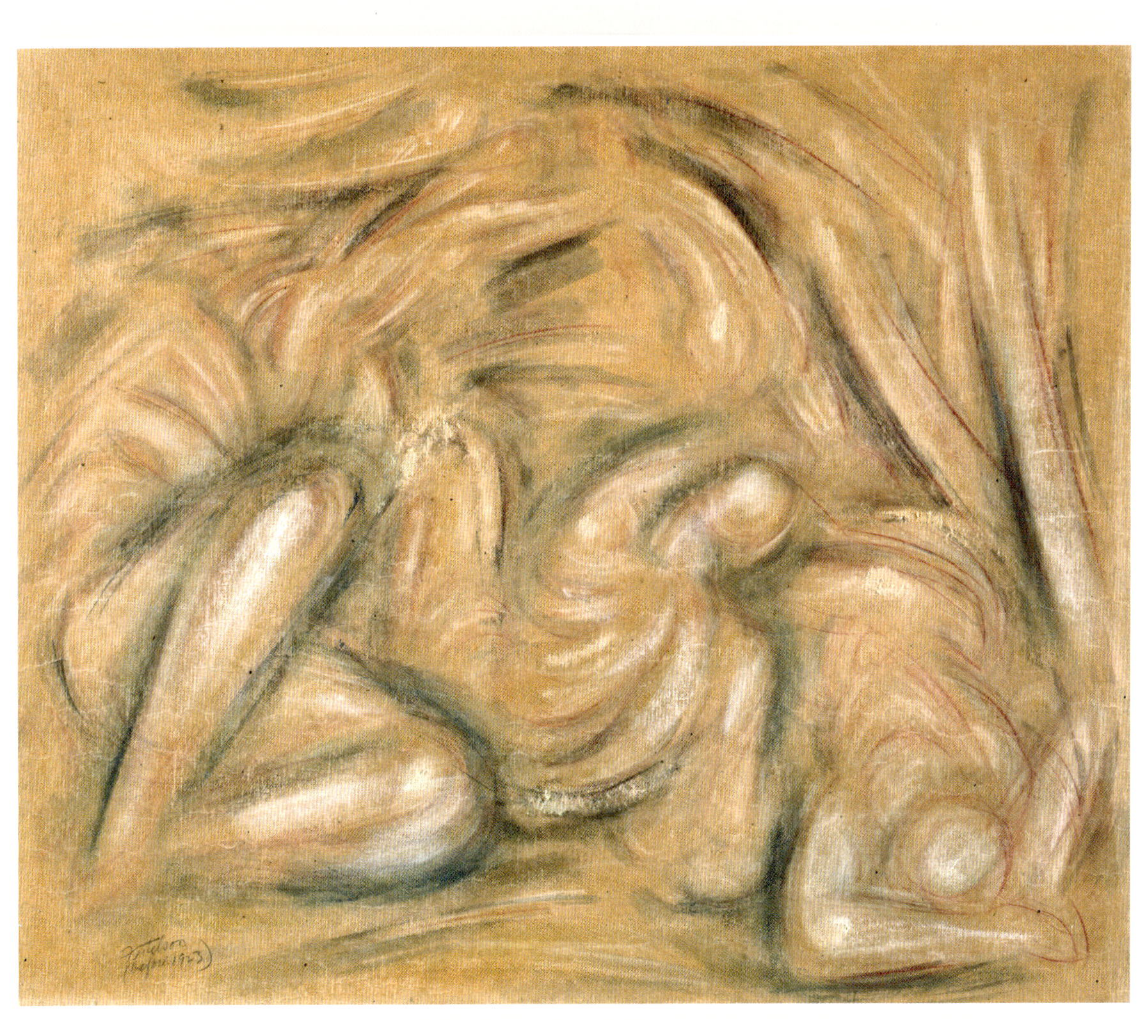

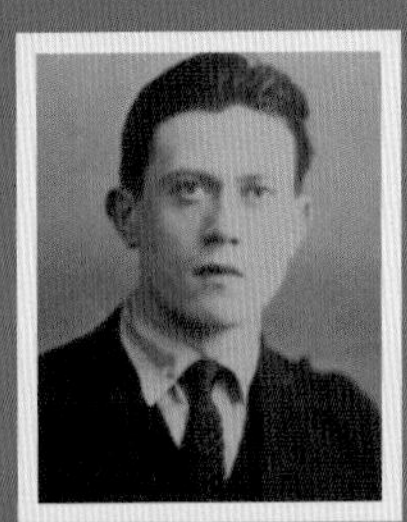

CHRONOLOGY

1898-1912 Born February 11, 1898, Savannah, Georgia. Family moves to New York City. Before the age of six, receives first lessons in figure drawing from his father whose analytical approach makes a deep and lasting impression.
Exposed to works and reproductions of the masters as well as contemporary art in his father's extensive library and periodical collection. At age 12, begins painting in oils.

1913 At age 15, studies for a brief period under the tutelage of sculptor Karl Teft, whose analytical approach afftects him significantly. Uses Teft's systematic method to examine the articulation of form by Renaissance masters, particulary Michelangelo and Tintoretto.
Attends the Armory Show in New York, where he is impressed by the work of Cézanne, Duchamp, Matisse and Gauguin.
Also begins to study the work of Italian Futurists, particulary Boccioni. Through this intensive study Feitelson's "kinetic period" is born.

1916 Meets Robert Henri, founder of The Eight. Occupies a studio in Greenwich Village.

1917 Moves to a new studio above the Penguin Club on 15th Street. During these early years works alone and educates himself by visiting The Metropolitan Museum of Art. His work at this time reflects a vital synthesis of Cubism and Futurism. Meets Pascin at the Penguin Club.

1918 Meets Walter Pach, John Sloan and Arthur B. Davies.

1919 Visited by Gaston Lachaise.
Takes first trip to Paris and enrolls himself at the Académie Colarossi as an independent student in life drawing. During his stay in Paris, notes exhaustion of Cubism and revival of classicism.

1920 Returns to New York, moves into a studio on 14th Street. Sees work of Brancusi, most likely at the Société Anonyme. Impressed by the early work of Nadelman. Creates one square of a composite wall-hanging by The Eight, at the request of John Sloan. Continues to create kinetic works based on the life-drawings made while in Paris and New York.

1922 Returns to Paris. Aware that artists Picasso, Derain, Théophile Robert and others are working in a classical style; critics proclaim Cubism to be dead and Neoclassicism the new mode. Turns from kinetic organizations towards more formal figure compositions.
Travels through Italy and is re-inspired by the early Renaissance masters.

1923 Remains in Paris, but makes visits to Corsica, Italy; his sketches from this island will become the basis for later neo-classical works of peasant subjects.

1924 Returns to New York, occupying a studio on East 64th Street. Begins exhibiting at the Daniel Gallery and receives critical acclaim for his neo-classical painting, *Judgment of Paris*.

1925 Premiere solo exhibition at the Daniel Gallery, New York.

1925-26 Brooklyn Museum acquires Feitelson's large painting, *Diana at the Bath*.

1926-27 Returns to Paris and takes a studio on Rue de la Seine. Exhibits in the Salon d'Automne. Returns to the United States and travels to Los Angeles in November for a winter stay which becomes his permanent residence.

1928 Moves into a studio on Highland Avenue, in the heart of Hollywood.
Exhibits with Nathalie Newking at Wilshire Galleries, directed by an acquaintance of Winslow Homer. Premiere solo museum exhibition at the California Palace of the Legion of Honor, San Francisco. Solo exhibition at the Los Angeles County Museum of Art.
Meets Stanton Macdonald-Wright.

1929 Exhibits at the Los Angeles County Museum of Art with Conrad Buff, Nathalie Newking and Hanson Puthuff.
Teaches a summer painting course at the Chouinard Art Institute, Los Angeles.

1930 Formulates first ideas of Subjective Classicism, to be known as Post-Surrealism.
Los Angeles Times publishes Feitelson's article, *"Eclecticism…What Is It?"* on January 26th.
Hired as an instructor at the Stickney Hall School of Art in Pasadena, California.
Exhibits in a Neo-Classical show at the Brooklyn Museum, New York.
Meets art critic and writer, Jules Langsner.

1930-31 Ruben Kadish and Philip Goldstein (Philip Guston) are among Feitelson's students.

1932 Resides on DeLongpre Avenue in Hollywood. Los Angeles County Museum of Art acquires his painting, *Two Peasant Children*.

1933 Resides on Fountain Avenue in Hollywood. Exhibits at Los Angeles County Museum of Art, California Palace of the Legion of Honor, San Francisco.

1933/34 Stanley Rose and Murray Youlin open the first contemporary art gallery in Los Angeles at the Centaur bookshop on Selma near Vine in Hollywood. Feitelson directs and designs the gallery.

1934 Feitelson founds Subjective Classicism, or Post-Surrealism, with Helen Lundeberg.

The first Post-Surrealist exhibition is held at the Centaur Gallery in November, includes the work of Feitelson, Lundeberg, Labaudt, Merrild, Ret and Lehman. Creates murals for the Federal Public Works Art Project.

1935 Designs and directs the new Stanley Rose Gallery, organizing exhibits of Juan Gris, Carlos Merida, Post-Surrealists, Lundeberg, Kadish, Merrild and Goldstein (Guston). Leaves the Rose Gallery to direct the Hollywood Gallery of Modern Art, located across from the Egyptian Theatre.
Along with Alexander Archipenko, juries a Modern Art Show.
Included in a Post-Surrealist show at the War Memorial Museum in San Francisco, which traveled to the Brooklyn Museum, New York.

1936 Included in a critically acclaimed Post-Surrealist exhibition at the Brooklyn Museum, New York. Exhibits in *Fantastic Art: Dada and Surrealism*, Museum of Modern Art, New York, through 1937.

1936/37 Begins work on the Los Angeles County Hall of Records mural for the California Works Progress Administration Federal Art Project (WPA/FAP).

1937 Moves to studio on Western Avenue just north of Melrose where he will remain for ten years. Appointed Supervisor of Murals, Paintings and Sculpture for Southern California, Federal Art Project. Exhibits in the *School of Paris* show at the Stendahl Galleries, Los Angeles. Exhibits at the Whitney Museum of American Art, New York, in 1937 *Exhibition of Contemporary American Art*.

1938 Two of Feitelson's murals are shown at Los Angeles County Museum of Art and three more murals are completed for The Thomas Edison School.

1939 Lithograph, *Reading*, is included in the New York World's Fair. Begins directing exhibitions with Helen Wurdemann at the Los Angeles Art Association. Lithograph, *Post-Surrealist Configuration: Biological Symphony* is exhibited at the Whitney Annual, New York.

1942 United States enters World War II. WPA/ FAP begins to limit operations. Begins romantic paintings of an introspective, subjective nature.

1943 WPA/FAP officially ends.

1944 Begins teaching at the Art Center School, Los Angeles. Solo exhibition at the Los Angeles County Museum of Art and the San Francisco Museum of Art, featuring romantic paintings and his first abstract paintings, *Post-Surrealist Configurations*, later to be called *Magical Space Forms*. Virginia Museum of Fine Arts includes Feitelson in the *Fourth Biennial Exhibit of Contemporary American Painting*.

1945 Incorporates principles of abstraction in his courses at the Art Center School.

1947 Becomes director of the Gallery of Mid-20th Century Art on Clark Street, in Los Angeles. Exhibits at the Art Institute of Chicago in *Abstract and Surrealist American Art*.
Exhibits at the Pasadena Institute of Art, California, in *Eighteen California Artists*.
Moves to Clark Street in Los Angeles.
Organizes exhibits at the Mid-20th Century Gallery that include De Chirico, Leonor Fini, Eugene Berman, Helen Lundeberg, Lepri, Brauner, Jacques Herold and Matta, et al.

1948 Organizes a Stanton Macdonald-Wright exhibition at the Art Center School Galleries.
Paints first *Magical Space Form*, exploring for the first time the ambiguity of space/form which becomes the predecessor of hard-edge abstraction. Moves to Westwood Boulevard in Los Angeles.

1949 Exhibits and lectures widely in Southern California and San Francisco. Moves to studios on Ardmore Street in Los Angeles.

1950 Exhibits at the University of Illinois and in Los Angeles.
Paints several small paintings in which he uses the bisected format and manipulation of space within the frame. These works presage his later *Dichromatic Organizations* of the late 1950s through 1960s.

1951 Named *Carnegie Visiting Professor*, University of Illinois, Urbana.
Exhibits *Magical Space Forms*, 1951 (68 x 100 inches), at the Los Angeles Art Association, bridging his *Magical Forms* and *Magical Space Forms* series.
Exhibits in *Contemporary Painting in the United States* at the Los Angeles County Museum of Art.
Juries several exhibitions in Southern California.
For the first time, uses plain, primed canvas in a painting.
Serves as a juror and is included in the exhibition, *American Watercolors, Drawings and Prints* at the Metropolitan Museum of Art, New York.
Moves to studios on 3rd Street in Los Angeles in September.
Functionists West group exhibits for the first time at the Los Angeles Art Association, featuring originators Feitelson, Helen Lundeberg, Stephen Longstreet and Elise Cavanna.

1952 Retrospective exhibition at the Pasadena Art Institute, California, is a critical success.

1953 Exhibits at the Colorado Springs Fine Art Center, Colorado.
Second exhibit of the *Functionists West* group with fourteen

new members.
Completes a *Stripe* painting, which derives from ideas taught to students at the Art Center School of Design, using color and spacing to create visual activity.

1955 Thirty year retrospective at the McNay Art Institute, San Antonio, Texas.
Exhibits in the Whitney Annual, New York.
Exhibits in the 3rd Biennial of São Paulo, Brazil.

1956 Begins a successful television series on NBC entitled *Feitelson on Art*, which lasts through 1963.

1958 Exhibits at the University of Nebraska Art Galleries in Lincoln. Exhibits with Helen Lundeberg at Scripps College, Claremont, California.
Participates in *Black and White Exhibition*, curated by Jules Langsner in Los Angeles.

1959 Organizes and leads a meeting of Abstract Classicists, including Karl Benjamin, Frederick Hammersley, John McLaughlin, with the critic Jules Langsner.
The landmark exhibition, *Four Abstract Classicists* is held at the Los Angeles County Museum of Art. Organized by Jules Langsner, this show travels to the San Francisco Museum. Later, a revised version under the title of *West Coast Hard Edge* travels to London (Institute of Contemporary Art) and Belfast, Ireland (Queens College).
Exhibits in *50 Paintings by 37 Painters of the Los Angeles Area* at the University of California, Los Angeles, Art Galleries, curated by Henry Hopkins.
Begins to exhibit at the Paul Rivas Gallery, Los Angeles.
Uses masking tape for the first time to create sharp edges in his paintings.

1961 Exhibits in Auckland, New Zealand.

1962 Exhibits in *Geometric Abstraction* in America at the Whitney Museum of American Art, New York.
Solo exhibition at the Long Beach Museum of Art, California. Introduces curvilinear forms, which remain the prominent motif in future work.
Joins the Ankrum Gallery in Los Angeles.

1962-63 Museum of Modern Art, New York, acquires and exhibits Feitelson's painting, *Magical Space Forms, 1955*.
Exhibits at the Whitney Museum, the Walker Art Center, the Albright-Knox Art Gallery and the Des Moines Art Center in *Fifty California Artists*, organized by San Francisco Museum with assistance from the Los Angeles County Museum of Art.

1963 Begins first paintings of pure lines, which, by 1965 become the major pictorial element in his painting.

1964 Exhibits at Phoenix Art Museum, Arizona.

1965 Exhibits at the Museum of Modern Art, New York, in *The Responsive Eye*. Exhibits at the Whitney Annual, New York, through January 1966.

1966 Exhibits at the Museum of Modern Art, New York, in the *Recent Aquisitions* show (Untitled, 1964).

1968 Joins the David Stuart Galleries, Los Angeles.

1969 Awarded honorary degree of Doctor of Fine Arts from the Art Center College of Design.

1969-71 Exhibits at the American Embassy, Moscow, in *American Contemporary Art*, organized by the Museum of Modern Art, New York.

1972 *Lorser Feitelson: A Retrospective Exhibition* is presented at the Los Angeles Municipal Art Gallery in August.
Named *Chairman Emeritus* of the Fine Arts Department, Art Center College of Design.

1973 Honored by the Otis Art Institute, Los Angeles, as a Distinguished American Artist.

1974 Included in *Nine Senior Southern California Painters*, the opening exhibition of the Los Angeles Institute of Contemporary Art.

1976 Exhibits in *Painting and Sculpture in California: The Modern Era*, at the San Francisco Museum of Modern Art.
The Oakland Museum, California, acquires Feitelson's line painting, *Untitled*, 1969.

1977 Exhibits at the Los Angeles County Museum of Art.
Exhibits at the National Collection of Fine Art, the Smithsonian Institution, Washington, D.C.
David Stuart Galleries presents a solo exhibition of Feitelson's early works.

1978 Feitelson dies on May 24th of heart failure brought on by a recent illness.

Information compiled from:
Moran, Diane Degasis.
The Painting of Lorser Feitelson. Diss.
University of Virginia. 1979.

1925   The Daniel Gallery, New York.
1926   Neumann Galleries, New York.
        Salon d'Automne, Paris.
        Dudensing Galleries, New York, 1926-27.
1928   California Palace of the Legion of Honor, San Francisco.
        Los Angeles County Museum, California.
        Wilshire Gallery, Los Angeles, California.
1931   Fine Arts Gallery of San Diego, California.
1932   California Palace of the Legion of Honor, San Francisco.
        Ilsley Galleries, Los Angeles, California.
1933   Ebell Salon, Los Angeles, California.
        Laguna Beach Art Association, California.
1935   Stanley Rose Gallery, Los Angeles, California.
1944   Los Angeles County Museum, California.
        San Francisco Museum of Art, California.
1947   Hartwell Galleries, Los Angeles, California.
1949   Art Center School Gallery, Los Angeles, California.
1952   Pasadena Art Institute, California.

SELECTED SOLO EXHIBITIONS

1955   Marion Koogler McNay Art Institute, San Antonio, Texas.
1958   Scripps College Art Galleries, Florence Rand Lang Art Building, Claremont, California.
1959   *Anna Mahler/Lorser Feitelson*, Paul Rivas Gallery, Los Angeles, California. Catalogue published.
1960   Paul Rivas Gallery, Los Angeles, California.
1961   Paul Rivas Gallery, Los Angeles, California.
1962   Long Beach Museum of Art, California.
        Ankrum Gallery, Los Angeles, California.
1963   Chapman College Purcell Art Association, Orange, California.
1964   Ankrum Gallery, Los Angeles, California.
1967   Occidental College, Los Angeles, California.
1968   *Feitelson, The Years of Vision: 1920-1950*, Los Angeles Art Association Galleries, California.
        Ankrum Gallery, Los Angeles, California.
1972   *Lorser Feitelson, A Retrospective Exhibition*, Municipal Art Gallery, Barnsdall Park, Los Angeles, California. Catalogue published.
        Lundeberg, Feitelson, First Showing: A Series of New Color Prints, Los Angeles Art Association Galleries, California.
1977   *Lorser Feitelson, Selection of Small Paintings*, David Stuart Galleries, Los Angeles, California.
1978   *Lorser Feitelson (1898-1978)* A Memorial Tribute, Whitney Museum of American Art, New York. Catalogue published.
1980-81 *Lorser Feitelson and Helen Lundeberg: A Retrospective Exhibition*, San Francisco Museum of Modern Art, California.
        Catalogue published. Also shown at The Frederick S. Wight Art Gallery, University of Los Angeles, California.
1982   *Lorser Feitelson Paintings 1964-1971*, Jan Baum Gallery, Los Angeles, California.
1983   Tobey C. Moss Gallery, Los Angeles, California.
1987   *Lorser Feitelson: Magical Space Forms, Boulder Series*, Tobey C. Moss Gallery, Los Angeles, California. Catalogue published.
1988   *Lorser Feitelson 1895-1978*, Tobey C. Moss Gallery, Los Angeles, California. Catalogue published.
1989   *Lorser Feitelson: Artist / Teacher*, Long Beach City College, Fine Arts Gallery, California.
        The Kinetic Line, Lorser Feitelson, University of California, Riverside, University Art Gallery.
1990   *Lorser Feitelson: Exploration of the Figure, 1919-1929*, Monterey Peninsula Museum of Art, California.
        Lorser Feitelson: The Organic Line: 1916-1977, Tobey C. Moss Gallery, Los Angeles, California.
1992   *Lorser Feitelson: Motion as Line*, Tobey C. Moss Gallery, Los Angeles, California.
1995   *Lorser Feitelson / John McLaughlin: Abstract Classicists*, Tobey C. Moss Gallery, Los Angeles, California.
1996   *Lorser Feitelson: The Romantic Years 1919-1949*, Tobey C. Moss Gallery, Los Angeles, California.
1998   *Lorser Feitelson: Magical Forms to Hard Edge*, Tobey C. Moss Gallery, Los Angeles, California.
2001   *Lorser Feitelson*, Patricia Faure Gallery, Santa Monica, California. Catalogue published.
2003   *Lorser Feitelson and the Invention of Hard Edge Painting 1945-1965*, Louis Stern Fine Arts, West Hollywood, CA.
        Catalogue Published.

SELECTED GROUP EXHIBITIONS

1924   *A Group of Modern Painters*, The Daniel Gallery, New York. Catalogue published.

1926   *Independents Exhibition*, New York.

1927   *Whitney Studio Club Exhibition*, New York.

1928   *Ninth Annual Exhibition of Painting and Sculpture*, Los Angeles Museum. Catalogue published.

1929   *Conrad Buff, Lorser Feitelson, Nathalie Newking, Hanson Puthuff*, Los Angeles County Museum. Catalogue published.
         Tenth Annual Exhibition of Painting and Sculpture, Los Angeles County Museum. Catalogue published.

1930   *Eleventh Annual Exhibition of Painting and Sculpture*, Los Angeles County Museum. Catalogue published.

1932   *Thirteenth Annual Exhibition of Painting and Sculpture*, Los Angeles County Museum. Catalogue published.

1933   *Fourteenth Annual Exhibition of Painting and Sculpture*, Los Angeles County Museum. Catalogue published.
         Progressive Painters of Southern California, Palace of the Legion of Honor, San Francisco, California. Catalogue published.
         Progressive Painters of Southern California, Fine Arts Gallery of San Diego, California. Catalogue published.

1934   *Fifteenth Annual Exhibition of Painting and Sculpture*, Los Angeles County Museum. Catalogue published.
         Paintings by California Modernists, Foundation of Western Art, Los Angeles. Catalogue published.
         Progressive Painters of Southern California, Los Angeles County Museum. Catalogue published.
         Public Works of Art Project, 14th Region Southern California, Los Angeles County Museum.
         Group Exhibition, El Capitan College of the Theatre, Los Angeles.
         Surrealisme & Post-Surrealisme (New Classicism), Centaur Gallery, Los Angeles.

1935   *Fifty-Fifth Annual Exhibition of the San Francisco Art Association*, San Francisco Museum of Art
         Catalogue published under title "Opening Exhibition."
         Post Surrealist Exhibition, San Francisco Museum of Art, California. Also shown at The Brooklyn Museum,
         New York under title "Postsurrealism."
         Post-Surrealists and Other Moderns, Stanley Rose Gallery, Los Angeles.
         Group Exhibition, Hollywood Gallery of Modern Art, Los Angeles.

1936   *Fantastic Art, Dada, Surrealism*, Museum of Modern Art, New York. Catalogue published.
         Oil Painting and Water Colors by California Artists, also known as "The Post Surrealist Show," Brooklyn Museum, New York.

1937   *1937 Annual Exhibition of Contemporary American Painting*, Whitney Museum of American Art, New York. Catalogue published.

1938   *Post Surrealism*, Stendahl Galleries, Los Angeles.

1939   *All California Painting and Sculpture Exhibition*, Los Angeles County Museum.
         Southern California Art Project, Los Angeles County Museum. Catalogue published.

1940   *California Creates*, Stendahl Galleries, Los Angeles. Also shown at San Francisco Museum of Art.
         1940 Exhibition of Contemporary American Art, Whitney Museum of American Art, New York. Catalogue published.

1944   *The Fifty-Fifth Annual Exhibition: Watercolors and Drawings*, The Art Institute of Chicago. Catalogue published.
         The Fourth Biennial Exhibit of Contemporary American Painting, Virginia Museum of Fine Arts.

1945   *The First Biennial Exhibition of Drawings by American Artists*, Los Angeles County Museum. Catalogue published.
         Group Exhibition, Fitzsimmons Studio, Los Angeles.

1946   *Paintings of the Year*, National Academy of Design, New York. Catalogue published.

1947   *Abstract and Surrealist American Art*, The Art Institute of Chicago. Catalogue published.
         Eighteen California Artists, Pasadena Institute of Art, California.

1949   *California Centennials Exhibition of Art*, Los Angeles County Museum. Catalogue published.
         Ninth Invitational Purchase Prize Art Exhibition, Chaffey Community Art Association, Ontario, California. Catalogue published.
         Exhibition of Contemporary American Painting, University of Illinois, College of Fine and Applied Arts, Urbana. Catalogue published.

1950   *Sixth Annual Exhibition by the Artists of Los Angeles and Vicinity*, Municipal Art Commission and the Los Angeles City Council,
         shown at the Greek Theatre. Catalogue published.
         Exhibition of Contemporary American Painting, University of Illinois, College of Fine and Applied Arts, Urbana. Catalogue published.

1951   *146th Annual Exhibition of Painting and Sculpture*, Pennsylvania Academy of Fine Arts.

1951   *Annual Exhibition of Contemporary Painting in the United States*, Los Angeles County Museum. Catalogue published.
         Seventh Annual Exhibition by the Artists of Los Angeles and Vicinity, Municipal Art Commission and the Los Angeles City Council,
         shown at the Greek Theatre. Catalogue published.
         Portable Murals, Los Angeles Art Association Galleries.
         Exhibition of Contemporary American Painting, University of Illinois, College of Fine and Applied Art, Urbana. Catalogue published.

1952   *American Water Colors, Drawings and Prints/ A National Competitive Exhibition*, The Metropolitan Museum of Art, New York.
         Catalogue published.

1953   *Fourteen Artists West of the Mississippi*, Colorado Springs Fine Arts Center, Colorado. Catalogue published.

1954   *Functionists West*, Los Angeles Art Association Galleries.

1955   *Annual Exhibition: Paintings, Sculpture, Watercolors, Drawings*, Whitney Museum of American Art, New York. Catalogue
         published.
         III Bienal de São Paulo, Museu de Arte Moderna de São Paulo, Brazil. Catalogue published. United States section organized by San Francisco
         Museum of Art. Catalogue published under the title *Pacific Coast Art, United States' Representation at the IIIrd Biennial of São Paulo*.

1958   *Artists Invite Artists*, Esther Robles Gallery, Los Angeles.
        Sixty–Eighth Annual Exhibition, University of Nebraska Art Galleries, Lincoln. Catalogue published.
1959   *Four Abstract Classicists*, Los Angeles County Museum. Catalogue published. Also shown at San Francisco Museum of Art.
        Revised version shown at Institute of Contemporary Art, London, England and Queens College, Belfast, Ireland, under the title
        West Coast Hard Edge 1960.
        1949/1959 A Decade in the Contemporary Galleries, Pasadena Art Museum, California. Catalogue published.
        Fifty Paintings by Thirty Seven Painters of Los Angeles Area, San Francisco Museum of Art, California. Catalogue published.
1961   *The Nude in American Painting*, The Brooklyn Museum, New York. Catalogue published.
        Painting from the Pacific: Japan, America, Australia, New Zealand, Auckland City Art Gallery, New Zealand. Catalogue published.
1962   *The Artist's Environment: West Coast*, The Amon Carter Museum of Western Art, Forth Worth, Texas. Catalogue published.
        Also shown at the UCLA Art Galleries, Los Angeles; Oakland Museum of Art, California.
        Fifty California Artists, Whitney Museum of American Art, New York. Catalogue published. Organized by San Francisco
        Museum of Art with assistance of Los Angeles County Museum of Art. Also shown at Walker Art Center, Minneapolis, Minnesota;
        Albright-Knox Art Gallery, Buffalo, New York; Des Moines Art Center, Iowa.
        Geometric Abstraction in America, Whitney Museum of American Art, New York. Catalogue published.
1963   *Arts of Southern California-XIV: Early Moderns*, Long Beach Museum of Art, California. Catalogue published.
1964   *California Hard Edge Painting*, Pavilion Gallery, Balboa, California. Catalogue published.
        1964 Festival of Fine Arts/Art and Anti-Art, Occidental College, Los Angeles. Catalogue published.
        Of Time and the Image, Ankrum Gallery Artists, Phoenix Art Museum, Arizona. Catalogue published.
        Southern California Original Hard Edge Painters, Esther Robles Gallery, Los Angeles.
1965   *Colorists 1950-1965*, San Francisco Museum of Art, California. Catalogue published.
        1965 Annual Exhibition of Contemporary American Painting, Whitney Museum of American Art, New York. Catalogue published.
        The Responsive Eye, The Museum of Modern Art, New York. Catalogue published. Also shown at City Art Museum of St. Louis,
        Missouri; Seattle Art Museum, Washington; Pasadena Art Museum, California; The Baltimore Museum of Art, Maryland.
        Twelfth Exhibition of Contemporary American Painting and Sculpture, Krannert Art Museum, University of Illinois, Champaign.
        Catalogue published.
        Eighteenth Annual Creative Arts Exhibition, Henderson Fine Arts Gallery, University of Colorado.
1966   *1966 Invitational, California '66 Painters and Sculptors*, E.B. Crocker Art Gallery, Sacramento, California. Catalogue published.
        New Modes in California Painting and Sculpture, La Jolla Museum of Art, California. Catalogue published.
        Contemporary California Art from the Lytton Collection, Lytton Center of The Visual Arts, Los Angeles. Catalogue published.
        The Search/Ten Leading California Artists in Pursuit of a Personal Vision, Lytton Center of the Visual Arts, Los Angeles. Catalogue published.
1967   *Artists' Artists*, Lytton Center of the Visual Arts, Los Angeles. Catalogue published.
        Cubism, Its Impact in the USA, 1910-1930, sponsored by University of New Mexico Art Museum and Junior League of
        Albuquerque. Catalogue published. Also shown at Marion Koogler McNay Art Institute, San Antonio, Texas; San Francisco
        Museum of Art, California; Los Angeles Municipal Art Gallery.
        1967 Annual Exhibition of Contemporary American Painting, Whitney Museum of American Art, New York. Catalogue published.
        West Coast Invitational, 1967, E.B. Crocker Art Gallery, Sacramento, California. Catalogue published.
1968   *1968 Invitational, West Coast '68 Painters and Sculptors*, E.B. Crocker Art Gallery, Sacramento, California. Catalogue published.
        Group Exhibition, David Stuart Galleries, Los Angeles.
1969   *Color in Control*, Museum of Fine Arts, St. Petersburg, Florida. Catalogue published. Also shown at the Loch Haven Art Center, Orlando, Florida.
        Microcosm '69, Long Beach Museum of Art, California. Catalogue published.
        West Coast 1945-1969, Pasadena Art Museum, California. Catalogue published.
        Group Exhibition, David Stuart Galleries, Los Angeles.
1970   *American Contemporary Art*, organized under the auspices of the International Council at the Museum of Modern Art, New York.
        Also shown at the American Embassy, Moscow. Catalogue published in Russian and English.
        American Painting 1970, Virginia Museum, Richmond.
        A Century of California Painting 1870-1970, E.B. Crocker Art Gallery, Sacramento, California. Catalogue published.
        Looking West, 1970, Joslyn Art Museum, Omaha, Nebraska. Catalogue published.
        Group Exhibition, David Stuart Galleries, Los Angeles.
1972   *Los Angeles Painters of the Nineteen-Twenties*, Pomona College Gallery, Montgomery Art Center, Claremont, California.
        Catalogue published.
        Group Exhibition, Los Angeles Municipal Gallery, Barnsdall Park.
        West Coast Art from the Permanent Collection, Pasadena Art Museum, California.
        Renewal Art of the 1930's-1940's: Southern California Artists, Los Angeles Art Association Galleries.
1974   *Nine Senior Southern California Painters*, Los Angeles Institute of Contemporary Art. Catalogue published in Los Angeles
        Institute of Contemporary Art *Journal*, December 1974 pages 45-53.
1975   *Avant-Garde Painting and Sculpture in America 1910-1925*, Delaware Art Museum, Wilmington, Delaware. Catalogue published.
1976   *American Artists '76: A Celebration*, Marion Koogler McNay Art Institute, San Antonio, Texas. Catalogue published.

1974   *Nine Senior Southern California Painters*, Los Angeles Institute of Contemporary Art. Catalogue published in Los Angeles
        Institute of Contemporary Art *Journal*, December 1974 pages 45-53.
1975   *Avant-Garde Painting and Sculpture in America 1910-1925*, Delaware Art Museum, Wilmington, Delaware. Catalogue published.
1976   *American Artists '76: A Celebration*, Marion Koogler McNay Art Institute, San Antonio, Texas. Catalogue published.
        Los Angeles: A Continuing Frontier 1940-1961, Occidental College Gallery, Los Angeles.
        New Deal Art: California, de Saisset Art Gallery and Museum, University of Santa Clara, California. Catalogue published.
        Painting and Sculpture in California: The Modern Era, San Francisco Museum of Modern Art, California. Catalogue published.
        Also shown at National Collection of Fine Arts, Smithsonian Institution, Washington D.C.
        Symbolism, Los Angeles Art Association Galleries.
1977   *Los Angeles Hard-Edge: The Fifties and Seventies*, Los Angeles County Museum of Art. Catalogue published under the title
        of "California: 5 Footnotes to Modern Art History."
        Surrealism and American Art: 1931-1947, Rutgers University Art Gallery, New Brunswick, New Jersey. Catalogue published.
1978   *Selections from the Frederick Weisman Company Collection of California Art*, The Art Museum and Galleries, California State
        University, Long Beach, California. Catalogue published. Also shown at The Corcoran Gallery of Art, Washington D.C.;
        The Albuquerque Museum of Art, History and Science, New Mexico.
1979   *Black and White are Colors: Paintings of the 1950's-1970's*, Montgomery Art Gallery, Pomona College, California. Catalogue published.
1980   *50's Abstract: A Summary of Los Angeles Painting from 1957-1960*, Conejo Valley Art Museum, Thousand Oaks, California.
        Catalogue published.

SELECTED GROUP EXHIBITIONS

1982   *Drawings and Illustrations by Southern California Artists before 1950*, Laguna Beach Museum of Art, California. Catalogue published.
1984   *The Frederick Weisman Collection of California Art*, Museum of Contemporary Art, Los Angeles.
1985   *Colorforms*, Security Pacific National Bank, Gallery at the Plaza, Los Angeles. Also shown at Tobey C. Moss Gallery, Los Angeles.
1986   *Aspects of California Modernism 1920-1950*, Board of Governors of the Federal Reserve System, Washington D.C., Catalogue published.
1990-92 *Turning the Tide: Early Los Angeles Modernists 1920-1956*, Santa Barbara Museum of Art, California. Catalogue published. Also
        shown at Laguna Art Museum, California; Oakland Museum of Art, California; Marion Koogler McNay Art Institute, San Antonio,
        Texas; Nora Eccles Harrison Art Museum, Utah State University, Logan; Palm Springs Desert Museum, California.
1992   *California Painting: The Essential Modernist Framework*, California State University, Los Angeles. Also shown at California State
        University, San Bernardino, California.
1994   *Independent Visions: California Modernism*, Long Beach Museum of Art, California.
1995   *Pacific Dreams*, UCLA Hammer Museum of Art, Los Angeles. Also shown at Oakland Museum of Art, California. Catalogue published.
1997   *On the Edge of America: California Modernist Art*, Jack Rutberg Fine Arts, Los Angeles.
1999   *Gold Rush to Pop: 200 Years of California Art*, Orange County Museum of Art, California.
2000   *Four Abstract Classicists Plus One*, Tobey C. Moss Gallery, Los Angeles.
2001   *American Surrealism*, Thomas McCormick Gallery, Chicago. Catalogue published.
        California Modernism, Tobey C. Moss Gallery, Los Angeles.
        Four Abstract Classicists, Gary Snyder Fine Art, New York.
2002   *Post Surrealism*, Pasadena Museum of California Art, California. Catalogue published.
2002-03 *Post Surrealism*, Nora Eccles Harrison Museum of Art, Utah State University, Utah.
2003   *It's Not the Size that Counts: Treasures Big and Small*, Jack Rutberg Fine Art, Los Angeles, CA
2004   *Conversations with the Collection: A Selection from the Permanent Collection*, Long Beach Museum of Art, Long Beach, CA
2004-05 *The Figure in California Modernism*, Spencer John Helfen Fine Arts, Beverly Hills, CA.
2004-05 *The Los Angeles School*, Otis College of Art + Design, Los Angeles, CA
2005   *Surrealism USA*, National Academy Museum, New York, New York

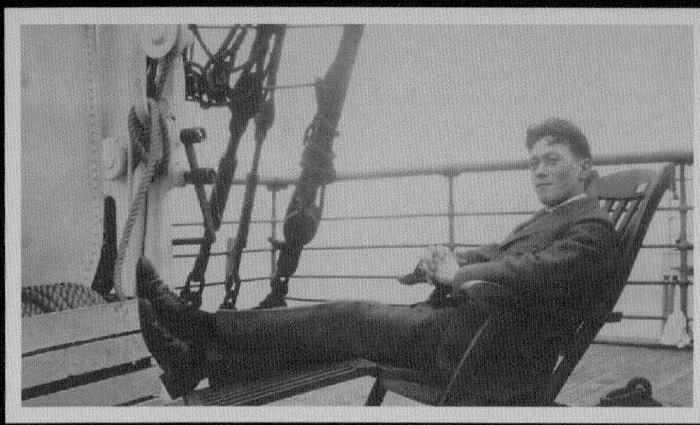

Lorser Feitelson aboard the S.S. Rochambeau, 1919

SELECTED PRIVATE COLLECTIONS

Herta and Paul Amir, Beverly Hills, CA.
Whitney Armstrong, New York, NY
Barry Berkus, Santa Barbara, CA
Francie F. Brody, Los Angeles, CA
The Buck Collection, Laguna Hills, CA
Mr. and Mrs. Harry Carmean, Santa Barbara, CA.
Dr. and Mrs. J. Thomas Chess, South Pasadena, CA.
Gloria Ellwood, Los Angeles, CA.
Betty Freeman, Beverly Hills, CA.
Murray Gribin, Beverly Hills, CA.
Mr. and Mrs. Victor Haboush, Brentwood, CA
June Harwood, Studio City, CA.
Allan Marion, Beverly Hills, CA.
Isabelle and John Marx, West Hollywood, CA
Mr. and Mrs. Alan C. Moss, Los Angeles, CA.
Mr. and Mrs. James Ries, Beverly Hills, CA.
Mark Seldis, Los Angeles, CA.
Mr. and Mrs. Russell Dymock Smith, Palos Verdes Estate, CA.
Gary Snyder, New York, NY
Roselyne Swig, San Francisco, CA.
Barbara and Sanford Wernick, West Hollywood, CA
Jennifer and Randy Wooster, Beverly Hills, CA

Brooklyn Museum of Art, New York, NY.
Joseph H. Hirshhorn Museum, Smithsonian Institution, Washington, D. C.
Honolulu Academy of Arts, HI.
Industrial Electronic Engineers, Los Angeles, CA.
James B. Lansing Sound. Inc., Los Angeles, CA.
Museum of Contemporary Art, San Diego, CA.
Library of Congress, Washington, D.C.
Long Beach Museum of Art, CA.
Los Angeles County Museum of Art, Los Angeles, CA.
Marion Koogler McNay Art Museum, San Antonio, TX.

COLLECTIONS

Mildred Lane Kemper Art Museum, St. Louis, MO.
Museum of Fine Arts, Boston, MA.
Museum of Modern Art, New York, NY.
National Bank of Omaha, Omaha, NE.
National Gallery of Art, Washington D.C.
Nora Eccles Harrison Museum of Art, Utah State University, Logan, UT.
Oakland Museum, CA.
Palm Springs Desert Museum, CA.
Phoenix Art Museum, AZ.
San Francisco Museum of Modern Art, CA.
Santa Barbara Museum of Art, CA.
Smithsonian American Art Museum, Washington, D. C.
Sheldon Memorial Art Gallery, Lincoln, NE.
University of Arizona Museum of Art, Tucson, AZ.
University of Virginia Art Museum, Charlottesville, VA.
Whitney Museum of American Art, New York, NY.
Frederick R. Weisman Foundation, Los Angeles, CA.
Zimmerli Art Museum, Rutgers University, NJ.

1.
SEATED FIGURE
IN ACTION
(KINETIC STUDY)
1917-18
wash on carton
10 1/8 x 13 3/4 inches
25.7 x 34.9 centimeters

2.
FIGURE
(KINETIC STUDY)
c. 1917-1918
watercolor on carton
4 x 5 1/2 inches
10.2 x 14 centimeters

3.
MOTHER AND CHILD
(KINETIC STUDY)
circa 1918
pastel and watercolor on carton
20 x 24 inches
50.8 x 61 centimeters

4.
TWO FIGURES
1918-19
oil on carton
9 x 12 inches
22.9 x 30.5 centimeters

5.
FIGURE GROUP
(STUDY IN KINETICS)
1918-19
oil on carton
11 1/2 x 27 inches
29.2 x 68.6 centimeters

6.
LEDA
(STUDY IN KINETICS)
1918-1919
oil on carton
24 x 26 inches
61 x 66 centimeters

7.
FIGURES
1918-1919
oil on carton
17 1/4 x 17 1/4 inches
43.8 x 43.8 centimeters

8.
BATHERS #8
1918-1919
oil on carton
16 x 20 inches
40.6 x 50.8 centimeters

9.
LANDSCAPE WITH
TWO FIGURES
1918-1919
watercolor and graphite on paper
9 x 12 inches
22.9 x 30.5 centimeters

10.
FIGURE
1918-1920
oil on carton
21 x 19 3/4 inches
53.3 x 50.2 centimeters

11.
THREE FIGURES
1919
Conte crayon on paper
9 1/4 x 11 1/4 inches
23.5 x 28.6 cm

12.
TWO NUDES
(MALE AND FEMALE)
1919
Conte crayon on paper
11 1/2 x 16 inches
29.2 x 40.6 centimeters

13.
NEW YORK BUILDINGS
1919
Conte crayon, wash and
gouache on paper
11 x 10 inches
27.9 x 25.4 centimeters

14.
MOTHER AND CHILD
1919
oil on carton
26 x 27 1/2 inches
66 x 69.9 centimeters

15.
TWO NUDES AND A CAT
1919
oil on carton
20 x 24 inches
50.8 x 61 centimeters

16.
TWO BATHERS
(ORGANIZED
ARTICULATION)
1919
oil on carton
23 x 28 inches
58.4 x 71.1 centimeters

17.
STUDY IN KINETICS
1919
oil on carton
24 1/2 x 19 3/4 inches
62.2 x 50.2 centimeters

18.
LEDA
(STUDY IN KINETICS)
1919
oil on carton
16 x 20 inches
40.6 x 50.8 centimeters

19.
LEDA (STUDY IN KINETICS)
1919
oil on carton
21 3/8 x 18 7/8 inches
54.5 x 47.8 centimeters

20.
SEATED FEMALE FIGURE
(KINETIC STUDY)
1919
Conte crayon on paper
11 x 13 inches
27.9 x 33 centimeters

21.
STUDY FOR LEDA
(STUDY IN KINETICS)
1919
graphite on paper
9 x 12 inches
22.9 x 30.5 centimeters

22.
LEDA
(STUDY IN KINETICS)
1919
graphite on paper
9 x 12 inches
22.9 x 30.5 centimeters

23.
FIGURE
(KINETIC ORGANIZATION)
1919-20
oil on carton
28 1/2 x 22 3/4 inches
72.4 x 57.8 centimeters

24.
KINETIC FIGURE
1919-20
oil on carton
30 x 24 inches
76.2 x 61 centimeters

25.
TWO BATHERS
(KINETIC STUDY)
1919-20
Oil on carton
20 x 16 inches
50.8 x 40.6 centimeters

26.
TWO BATHERS
(KINETIC ORGANIZATION)
1919-20
oil on carton
29 x 22 3/4 inches
73.7 x 57.8 centimeters

27.
MOTHER AND CHILD
(BATHERS, KINETIC
ORGANIZATION)
1919-1920
Oil on carton
12 x 14 inches
30.5 x 35.6 centimeters

28.
TWO BATHERS
(KINETIC STUDY)
1919-1920
oil on carton
18 1/2 x 13 1/4 inches
47 x 33.7 centimeters

29.
ARCHITECTURAL
ABSTRACTION-BUILDINGS
1920
watercolor and pencil on paper
14 x 11 inches
35.6 x 27.9 centimeters

30.
FEMALE FIGURE
SEATED AT TABLE
circa 1920
Pencil and watercolor on carton
11 x 8 inches
27.9 x 20.3 centimeters

31.
STILL LIFE
(2 PEARS, APPLE)
circa 1920
charcoal and oil pastel on paper
8 1/2 x 11 1/2 inches
21.6 x 29.2 centimeters

32.
STILL LIFE
(2 APPLES, PEAR)
circa 1920
charcoal and oil pastel on paper
8 3/4 x 11 3/8 inches
22.2 x 28.9 centimeters

33.
PEARS AND APPLES
1920
oil on carton
9 x 12 inches
30.5 x 22.9 centimeters

34.
INTERIOR
1921
Conte crayon on paper
21 x 17 1/4 inches
53.3 x 43.8 centimeters

35.
FEMALE FIGURE
1921
oil pastel and Conte
crayon on paper
10 3/8 x 6 inches
26.4 x 15.2 centimeters

CHECKLIST

36.
BATHERS
(KINETIC COMPOSITION)
before 1923
oil on carton
20 x 24 inches
50.4 x 59.7 centimeters

BY LORSER FEITELSON

"The Neo-Classic Movement." *The Argus* (San Francisco), May 1928, p. 8.

"Eclecticism – What is it?" *Los Angeles Times*, 26 January 1930, III, p. 24.

"What is Postsurrealism?" *Spanish Village Art Quarterly* (San Diego), Spring 1941, p. 6.

Introduction to *S. Macdonald-Wright, 35 Years of Creative Painting*. Los Angeles: The Art Center School Gallery, 1948. Reprinted in "Tributes to Stanton Macdonald-Wright." *American Art Review*, January-February 1974, p. 54.

Statement in *University of Illinois Exhibition of Contemporary American Painting*. Urbana: College of Fine and Applied Arts, 1950, p. 173.

Statement in *University of Illinois Exhibition of Contemporary American Painting*. Urbana: University of Illinois Press, 1951, p. 176.

ON LORSER FEITELSON

Lorser [Motion Picture]. Los Angeles: David O. Pfiel, 1972.

Lorser Feitelson Papers. Archives of American Art, Smithsonian Institution.

Feitelson, Lorser. Interview conducted by Betty Hoag. Archives of American Art, Smithsonian Institution, 12 May and 9 June 1964, 17 March 1965: microfilm 3419.

Feitelson, Lorser. Interview conducted by Fidel Danieli, Oral History Program. University of California, Los Angeles 1974.

Moran, Diane Degasis. "The Painting of Lorser Feitelson". Ph.D. dissertation, University of Virginia, 1979.

Lorser Feitelson and the Invention of Hard Edge Painting 1945-1965. Louis Stern Fine Arts, exhibition catalogue. West Hollywood: Louis Stern Fine Arts, 2003.

GENERAL WORKS

The Artist in America. [Compiled by the Editors of *Art in America*]. New York: Norton, 1967, pp. 231,251.

Ashton, Dore. *Yes, but... A Critical Study of Philip Guston*. New York: Viking Press, 1976, pp. 19-20, 22,23.

Baur, John I. H. *Revolution and Tradition in Modern American Art*. Cambridge: Harvard University Press, 1951, p. 106, fig. 22.

Catalog of the Permanent Collection of Painting and Sculpture. San Francisco: San Francisco Museum of Art, 1970, pp. 40-41.

Cummings, Paul. *Dictionary of Contemporary American Artists*. New York: St. Martin's Press, 1977, pp. 186-187.

Humblet, Claudine. *La Nouvelle Abstraction Américaine 1950-1970*. Milan: Skira/Seuil, 2003, volume 1, pp.377-421.

Jean, Marcel. *The History of Surrealist Painting*. New York: Grove Press, 1960, p. 274.

Kahan, Mitchell Douglas. "Subjective Currents in American Painting of the 1930s". Ph.D. dissertation, City University of New York, 1983.

Mendelowitz, Daniel M. *A History of American Art*. New York: Holt, Rinehart, & Winston, 1970, pp. 456, 457.

Monro, Isabel Stevenson, and Kate M. Monro. *Index to Reproductions of American Paintings*. New York: H. W. Wilson, 1948, p. 232.

_____. *Index to Reproductions of American Paintings. First Supplement*. New York: H. W. Wilson, 1964, p. 164.

Moure, Nancy Dustin Wall. *Dictionary of Art and Artists in Southern California Before 1930*. Los Angeles: Dustin Publications, 1975, pp. 84-85.

_____, and Phyllis Moure. *Artists' Clubs and Exhibitions in Los Angeles Before 1930*. Los Angeles: Dustin Publications, 1975.

Munro, Eleanor. *Originals: American Women Artists*. New York: Simon & Schuster, 1979, pp. 170, 172, 174-176, 495n.

O'Connor, Francis V., ed. *Art for the Millions*. Boston: New York Graphic Society, 1973, p. 298.

Pellegrini, Aldo. *New Tendencies in Art*. New York: Crown Publishers Inc., 1966, pp. 40, 139, 148, 156.

Pierson, William H., Jr., and Martha Davidson, eds. *Arts of the United States, a Pictorial Survey*. New York: McGraw-Hill, 1960, pp. 79, 340.

Plagens, Peter. *Sunshine Muse: Contemporary Art on the West Coast*. New York: Praeger, 1974, pp. 18, 29, 117, 118.

Rickey, George. *Constructivism: Origins and Evolution*. New York: George Braziller, 1967, pp. 66,133.

Seuphor, Michel. *Abstract Painting: Fifty Years of Accomplishment from Kandinsky to the Present*. New York: Abrams, 1962, pp. 242, 304.

Smith, Lyn Wall, and Nancy Dustin Wall Moure. *Index to Reproductions of American Paintings*. Metuchen, N.J.: Scarecrow Press, 1977, p. 221.

Smith, Richard, C. *Utopia and Dissent: Art, Poetry, and Politics in California*. University of California Press, 1995.

Wechsler, Jeffrey and Greta Berman. *Realism and Realities: the OTHER SIDE of American Painting 1940-1960*. Rutgers, State University of New Jersey, 1981, pp. 149,150.

Wheeler, Daniel. *Art Since Mid-Century: 1945 to the Present*. New York: Vendome Press, 1991, p. 198.

Dervaux, Isabelle. *Surrealism USA*. National Academy Museum, exhibition catalogue. New York: Hatje Cantz Publishers, 2005, plates 23 and 24.

ARTICLES AND REVIEWS

1924 "Painters Form Lively Group: An Enjoyable Exhibition of Moderns at the Daniel Gallery." *The World* (New York), *Metropolitan*

Section, 17 February 1924, p. 7. Review.

1926 Watson, Forbes. "Properties and Experiments." *The Arts*, April 1926, p. 209.

1928 "Living Artists to the Fore." *Los Angeles Times*, 5 February 1928, Ill, p. 14. Review.

Millier, Arthur. "In Los Angeles Galleries." *The Argus* (San Francisco), March 1928, p. 8. Review.

Salinger, Jehanne Biétry. "In San Francisco Galleries." *The Argus* (San Francisco), September 1928, pp. 9, 12. Review.

1929 Millier, Arthur. "Springboards for Art." *Los Angeles Times*, 8 September 1929, Ill, p. 14. Review.

"News of the Art Worlds." *Los Angeles Times*, 4 August 1929, Ill, p. 18.

1930 "Brooklyn Museum Shows Neo-Classic Art." *Art Digest*, August 1930, p. 13. Review.

1937 Mac-Gurrin, Buckley. "Art Stuff– Of, by and for the People." *Rob Wagner's Script*, Los Angeles, 14 August 1937.

1938 Mac-Gurrin, Buckley. "Art Stuff – Block that Kick!" *Rob Wagner's Script*, Los Angeles, 7 May 1938.

1939 "Hitting High Spots of Midseason Art Show." *Los Angeles Times*, 12 March 1939, Ill. p. 8. Review.

1940 Millier, Arthur. "Lorser Feitelson." *California Arts and Architecture*, May 1940, p. 8.

1944 Macdonald-Wright, S. "Art Stuff." *Rob Wagner's Script* (Los Angeles), 22 January 1944, p. 22. Review.

Millier, Arthur. "Feitelson Shows His Work as 'Artist in Transition.'" *Los Angeles Times*, 6 February 1944, Ill, p. 5. Review.

1945 Millier, Arthur. "Woman Has Edge in Show of Drawings." *Los Angeles Times*, 7 January 1945, Ill, p. 4. Review.

SELECTED BIBLIOGRAPHY

"Seen in Club and Temple." *Los Angeles Times*, 28 December 1930, Ill, p. 6. Review.

"The Summer Exhibition." *Brooklyn Museum Quarterly*, October 1930, pp. 141, 143, 145.

1933 Merlin, Milton. "Books – Art – Drama." *Touring Topics*, July 1933, p. 32. Review.

Millier, Arthur. "Fresco, 'Neo-Classicism' and Some Fresh Talents." *Los Angeles Times*, 22 January 1933, II, p. 2. Review.

1934 Millier, Arthur. "New Developments in Southern California Painting." *The American Magazine of Art*, May 1934, pp. 244, 247.

____. "Surrealists Take Time by Forelock and Stage Exhibit." *Los Angeles Times*, 25 November 1934, II, p. 6. Review.

1935 "On a Mexican Wall". *Time*, 1 April 1935, pp. 46, 48.

"Paint, Theory, Prints Liven This Week's Art Exhibitions." *Los Angeles Times*, 29 September 1935, II, p. 7. Review.

1936 Clements, Grace. "New Content – New Form." *Art Front*, March 1936.

Jewell, Edward Alden. "Brisk Pace in Museums." *New York Times*, 17 May 1936, Sec. 9, p. 10. Review.

Mac-Gurrin, Buckley. "Home-made Art Movement Performs as Scheduled." *Rob Wagner's Script* (Los Angeles), 25 July 1936, p. 16.

Millier, Arthur. "Our Artists in Person: Lorser Feitelson." *Los Angeles Times*, 16 February 1936, Ill, p. 9.

"Postsurrealism, the Supermodern." *The Literary Digest*, 11 July 1936, p. 23. Review.

1947 Millier, Arthur. "Artists Here Go Beyond Things Seen." *Los Angeles Times*, 23 May 1947, Ill, p. 4. Review.

1948 "Feitelson Directs." *Art Digest*, 15 September 1948, p. 38.

Ross, Kenneth. "Gold Rush' 48." *Art News*, January 1948, pp. 16, 17.

1949 "Dual Show Seen in Works at Art Center Galleries." *Daily News* (Los Angeles), 16 July 1949, p. 21. Review.

Millier, Arthur. "Exhibit is Contrast of Vigor and Delicacy." *Los Angeles Times*, 17 July 1949, IV, p. 6. Review.

1951 "Bowron Sets Own Hearing in Art Row." *Citizen News* (Hollywood), October 1951, p. 1.

Langsner, Jules. "Art News From Los Angeles." *Art News*, December 1951, p. 63. Review.

1952 Langsner, Jules. "Art News From Los Angeles." *Art News*, November 1952, p. 50. Review.

____. "Art News From Los Angeles." *Art News*, November 1952, pp. 50. Review.

Millier, Arthur. "Abstract Works Star in Feitelson Exhibit." *Los Angeles Times*, 30 March 1952, IV, p. 6. Review.

____. "Pioneer in California." *Art Digest*, 1 April 1952, pp. 15-16. Review.

1953 Wight, Frederick S. "Los Angeles." *Art Digest*, 1 December 1953, pp. 18, 31. Review.

1954 Langsner, Jules. "Art News From Los Angeles." *Art News*, January 1954, p. 21. Review.

1955 Ames, Walter. "New Art Show Tones Up TV Screen." *Los*

Angeles Times, 6 October 1955, Ill., p. 5.

Macdonald-Wright, S. "Art News From Los Angeles." *Art News*, October 1955, pp. 8, 59. Reprinted in the Los Angeles Institute of Contempoary Art *Journal*, April-May 1975, pp. 44-45.

1956   Palmer, Zuma. "Feitelson's Art Series Finding An Audience." *Radio-Television*, 15 November 1956, p.10.

1958   Langsner, Jules. "This Summer in Los Angeles." *Art News*, Summer 1958, p. 58. Review.

Millier, Arthur. "Feitelson's Show Works." *Los Angeles Times*, 30 March 1958, V. p.7. Review.

1959   Frankenstein, Alfred. "Some Reassurance from Abstract Classicists." *San Francisco Chronicle*, 8 July 1959, p. 35. Review.

Kessler, Charles S. "Los Angeles: Abstract Classicists." *Arts*, December 1959, p. 23. Review.

Langsner, Jules. "Art News from Los Angeles." *Art News*, September 1959, p. 50. Review.

Tillim, Sidney. "What Happened to Geometry." *Arts*, June 1959, pp. 38, 44.

Wurdemann, Helen. "Variety in the Los Angeles Area." *Art in America*, Fall 1959, p. 129. Review.

1960   Alloway, Lawrence. "Classicism or Hard-Edge?" *Art International*, 4; 2-3 (1960), p. 60. Review.

1962   "Feitelson, Gerchik, Schifrin." *Artforum*, July 1962, pp. 20-25. Discussion with Arthur Secunda.

Cherry, Herman. "Letters." *Artforum*, August 1962, p.2. (Response to "Feitelson, Gerchik, Schifrin", above.)

Feitelson, Lorser. "Letters." *Artforum*, September 1962, p.2. (Reply from Feitelson to Herman Cherry's letter, above.)

Wilder, Mitchell. "A Stirring in the Pacific Paint Pot." *Saturday Review*, 20 October 1962, pp. 56, 58. Review.

Wurdemann, Helen. "Directors' Choice. Los Angeles: Feitelson, Wight, Jarvaise." *Art in America*, Winter 1962, p. 126.

1963   Langsner, Jules. "Permanence and Change in the Art of Lorser Feitelson." *Art International*, September 1963, pp. 73-76

Leider, Philip, and John Coplans. "West Coast Art: Three Images." *Artforum*, June 1963, pp. 22, 24. Review.

Millier, Arthur. "Art of our City." *Los Angeles*, June 1963, p. 54.

Wholden, Rosalind G. "Lorser Feitelson, Ankrum Gallery." *Artforum*, 1: 7 [1963], pp. 14,15. Review.

1964   Coplans, John. "Circle of Styles on the West Coast." *Art in America*, June 1964, pp. 32, 33, 36.

____. "Formal Art." *Artforum*, Summer 1964, pp. 42, 44.

____. "John McLaughlin, Hard Edge, and American Painting." *Artforum*, January 1964, p.31.

Ewalt, Mary. "Early Modern Paintings by California Artists, Long Beach Museum of Art." *Artforum*, February 1964, p. 12. Review.

Opliger, Curt. "Lorser Feitelson, Ankrum Gallery." *Artforum*, May 1964, pp. 14, 17. Review.

von Breton, Harriet. "Phoenix." *Artforum*, September 1964, p. 48. Review.

Weeks, H. J. "First Annual Pacific Art Classic, Van Nuys Savings and Loan Assoc." *Artforum*, November 1964, p. 18. Review.

1965   Barnes, Molly. "Group Show, Ankrum Gallery." *Artforum*, November 1965, p. 12. Review.

Wurdemann, Helen. "A Stroll on La Cienega." *Art in America*, October-November 1965. pp. 115, 116. Review.

1966   Davis, Douglas. "Look at Los Angeles Now-the New 'Second City' of Art." *The National Observer*, 9 May 1966, p. 24.

Kurzen, Estelle. "Los Angeles." *Artforum*, December 1966, p.60. Review.

Perkins, Constance M. "Los Angeles: The Way You Look at It." *Art in America*, March-April 1966, p. 144.

Seldis, Henry J. "Locals Get Chance in Lytton Exhibit." *Los Angeles Times*, 4 July 1966, V, p.13. Review.

Wilson, William. "Didactic Exhibit at Lytton Gallery." *Los Angeles Times*, 21 October 1966, p. 10. Review.

1967   Howell, Betje. "Perspective on Art." *Independent* (Beverly Hills), 17 Aujust 1967, Review.

1968   Lynes, Russell. "The Mesh Canvas." *Art in America*, May-June 1968, p. 43 and cover.

1970   Seldis, Henry J. "Lorser Feitelson." *Art International*, May 1970, pp. 48-52.

1971   Young, Joseph E. "Helen Lundeberg: An American Independent." *Art International*, September 1971, pp. 46, 47, 50, 72.

1972   Howell, Betje. "Overdue Lorser Feitelson Survey at Municipal." *Los Angeles Herald-Examiner*, 13 August 1972, p. F-8. Review.

Jacobson, Linda, and Marilyn Nix. "Lorser Feitelson Retrospective." *Artweek*, 9 September 1972, pp. 1, 12. Review.

Seldis, Henry J. "Pioneer Modernist: Forty-Five Years of Lorser Feitelson." *Los Angeles Times*, Calendar, 27 August 1972, pp. 51-52. Review.

Wilson, William. "Saving the W.P.A. Murals." *Los Angles Times*, 21 August 1972, IV, p.3.

____. "A New Life for Art on the New Deal." *Los Angles Times*, 4 May 1972, IV, pp. 3,15.

Young, Joseph E. "Lorser Feitelson and Los Angeles Modernism." *Artweek*, 21 October 1972, pp. 9-11.

1973   Plagens, Peter. "Before What Flowering? Thoughts on West Coast Art." *Artforum*, September 1973, p. 37.

1974   Danieli, Fidel. "Nine Senior Southern California Painters."

Los Angeles Institute of Contemporary Art *Journal*, October 1974, pp. 32-34.

Erzen, Jale Nejdet. "The Single Line Paintings of Lorser Feitelson." *Sourcebook*, November-December 1974, pp. 18-19.

Seldis, Henry J. "The Pioneer Modernists: A Sure Cure for Amnesia." *Los Angeles Times*, 8 December 1974, p. 102. Review.

Wortz, Melinda. "Nine Senior Los Angeles Artists." *Artweek*, 14 December 1974, pp. 1,16. Review.

1975   Danieli, Fidel. "Peter Krasnow: Pioneer Los Angeles Modernist." *Artweek*, 22 March 1975, p. 5.

Plagens, Peter. "The Soft Touch of Hard Edge." Los Angeles Institute of Contemporary Art *Journal*, April-May 1975, pp. 16-18.

Selz, Peter, June Harwood and Karl Benjamin. "Setting the Record Straight." Los Angeles Institute of Contemporary Art *Journal*, April-May 1975, pp. 11-15.

1976   Frankenstein, Alfred. "A Confrontation with the Modern Era." *San Francisco Chronicle*, World. 12 September 1976, pp. 33, 34. Review.

1977   Albright, Thomas. "California Art Since the 'Modern Dawn.'" *Art News*, January 1977, pp. 69, 70. Review. Gruen, John, ed. "Far-from-Last Judgments or, Who's Overrated Now? And Underrated." *Art News*, November 1977, pp. 112, 113.

Kramer, Hilton. "A Survey of California Art." *New York Times*, 19 June 1977, p. 27.

Moran, Diane Degasis. "On Lorser Feitelson." *Art International*, October-November 1977, pp. 16-17, 35-41.

St. John, Terry. "Two Pioneering Southern California Modernists." *ART (Art Guild of the Oakland Museum Association)*, May, June 1977, Volume 5, Number 3.

Wilson, William. "Art Walk." *Los Angeles Times*, 7 October 1977, IV, p. 16. Review.

Wortz, Melinda. "Five Footnotes to Modern Art History." *Art News*, January 1977, pp. 73, 75. Review.

1978   Harwood, June. "In Memorian: Lorser Feitelson." *Los Angeles Times*, 11 June 1978.

Wilson, William. "Abstract Painter Lorser Feitelson Dies." *Los Angeles Times*, 26 May 1978.

1979   Kramer, Hilton. "Art: Exponent of Hard-Edge Abstraction." *New York Times*, 5 January 1979, p. C16. Review.
Reprinted in *San Francisco Chronicle, World*, 14 January 1979, p. 51.

Seldis, Henry J. "Lorser Feitelson." *Art International*, May 1979, pp. 48-52.

1980   Albright, Thomas. "Hard Edge Modernists From Southern California." *Review*, 12 October 1980, pp. 14, 15.

Dunham, Judith L. "Lorser Feitelson and Helen Lundeberg: Collaborative Lives, Individual Achievement." *Artweek*, 1 November 1980, Volume 11, Number 36.

1981   "Galleries." *Los Angeles Times*, 8 May 1981, IV, p. 4.

Ianco-Starrels, Josine. "Pioneer Couple Share Billing." *Los Angeles Times*, 15 March 1981.

Stofflet, Mary. "Double View: Helen Lundeberg and Lorser Feitelson." *Images and Issues* 1, Number 4, Summer 1981, pp. 16-17.

Wilson, William. "Sensitive Palettes of Feitelson – Lundeberg." *Los Angeles Times*, 5 April 1981, pp. 1, 92.

1982   "The Galleries." *Los Angeles Times*, 3 December 1982, IV, p. 18. Review.

Moran, Diane Degasis. "Post-Surrealism: The Art of Lorser Feitelson and Helen Lundeberg." *Arts 57*, Number 4, December 1982, pp. 124-128.

Muchnic, Suzanne. "The Galleries." *Los Angeles Times*, 5 March 1982, IV, p.14. Review.

1983   "The Galleries." *Los Angeles Times*, 3 June 1983, VI, p.10. Review.

1985   Ianco-Starrels, Josine. "Art News." *Los Angeles Times*, 27 January 1985.

Ianco-Starrels, Josine. "Art News." *Los Angeles Times*, 25 August 1985.

McKenna, Kristine. "The Galleries." *Los Angeles Times*, 17 May 1985,IV, p.10. Review.

Muchnic, Suzanne. "Contrasting Exhibits with a Common Thread." *Los Angeles Times*, 10 February 1985, pp.91-92.

Muchnic, Suzanne. "'Colorforms': An Old-Fashioned Salute." *Los Angeles Times*, 3 June 1985, IV, pp. 1,6.

Welchman, John. "California Had Its Own Avant-Garde." *Artnews*. May 1985, pp. 105, 106.

1986   Ianco-Starrels, Josine. "Eight Million Stories." *Los Angeles Times*, 28 December, 1986, P.86. Review.

1987   McKenna, Kristine. "The Galleries." *Los Angeles Times*, 6 February 1987, IV. Review.

1988   de Lima Greene, Alison. "The Artist as Performer." *Arts Magazine*, November 1988, pp.55,56.

1990   Curtis, Cathy. "Feitelson's Serene and Anxious Forms." *Los Angeles Times*, 5 October 1990, p. 24. Review.

1991   Baker, Kenneth A. "California Abstractionists of the 1940s and 1950s." *Architectural Digest*, May 1991, pp. 66, 70, 74,76.

1996   Duncan, Michael. "What's Wrong With This Picture?" *LA Weekly*, 20-26 December 1996, pp. 62, 63.

Cover: *Leda (Study in Kinetics)*, detail (plate 18)

Photography by Ed Glendinning

Design: Lilla Hangay, Santa Ana, California
Printing: C & C Offset Printing Co., Ltd., Hong Kong, China
Prepress: iocolor, Seattle, Washington
Typeface: Kurosawa Sans, Versailles
Printed on Japanese white matte art

© Essay by Peter Selz

Edition of 6000

ISBN 0-9749421-3-8
Library of Congress Control Number: 2005927738

Printed in China

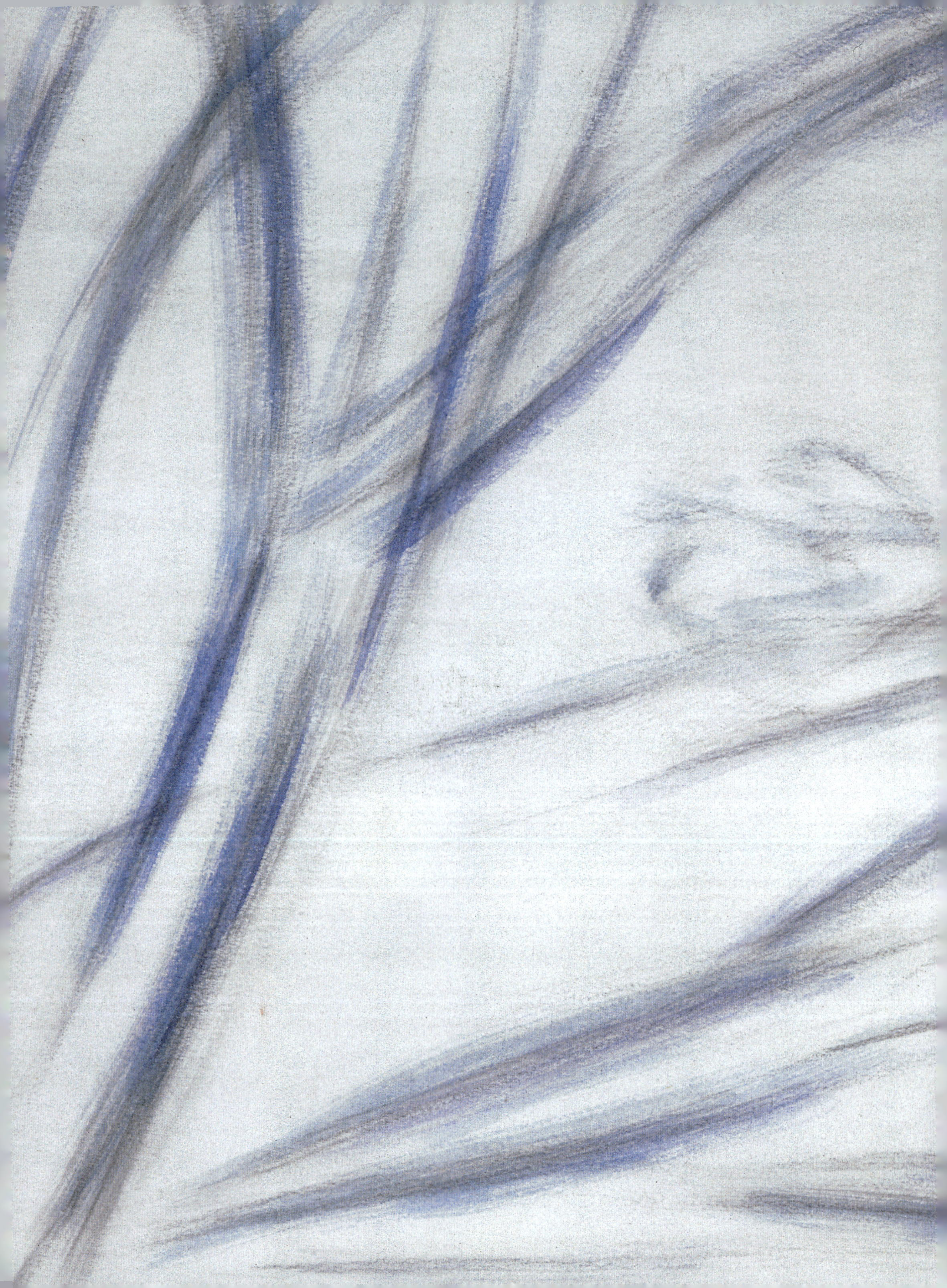